MASTERMIND GROUPS

ACCELERATORS OF SUCCESS

Published by:

Dilts Strategy Group
P. O. Box 67448
Scotts Valley CA 95067
USA
Phone: (831) 438-8314
E-Mail: info@diltstrategygroup.com
Homepage: http://www.diltstrategygroup.com

I.S.B.N. 978-1-947629-00-4

MASTERMIND GROUPS

ACCELERATORS OF SUCCESS

By:

Eric Baudet

Celine Baysselier

Olivier Christol

Christophe Genre-Jazelet

Nadia Grandclement

Catherine Pena

Laurent De Rauglaudre

Jean-François Thiriet

Translated from French by Barbara R. Cochran

Design and illustrations by: Antonio Meza

TABLE OF CONTENTS

TABLE OF CONTENTS

TABLE OF CONTENTS

TABLE OF CONTENTS

"It is literally true that you can succeed best and quickest by helping others to succeed."

- Napoleon Hill

"You are the average of the five people you spend the most time with."

- Jim Rohn

Acknowledgements

We want to thank Robert and Deborah Bacon Dilts for their inspiration and the support they lent to this writing project about collective intelligence. This book came about because of projects that were implemented at the time of the collective intelligence facilitator training in Avignon. Thanks to both of them for contributing to the momentum that collective intelligence is gaining internationally;

Giles Roy of Formation Évolution et Synergies, and the *Vision 2021*[1] association, for bringing together all of the goodwill that is part of the collective intelligence movement in France and throughout the world;

Colette Normandeau, Nick La Force, Xavier Lee, Karyn Greenstreet, Laurie Wann, Dorothy A. Martin-Neville, Yvonne Gerard, Alex Barker, and Dominique Le Martret for the passionate way they responded to our questions about their Mastermind group experience;

Antonio Meza for his illustrations, which liven up this book.

Thanks go out to all of those who will dare to become involved as Mastermind groups, as participants or facilitators, and who will contribute to the reconciliation of the egos and souls of entrepreneurs who have decided to take charge of their own lives.

---

[1]   www.vision-2021.fr

Preface

Mastermind Groups, Accelerators of success is a comprehensive, well-organized and pragmatic guidebook for how to create and facilitate an exciting and effective Mastermind Group. *Mastermind groups* are a new and evolving modality for promoting personal and professional growth that offer a combination of brainstorming, education, peer accountability and support in a group setting.

The concept of a Mastermind Group was initially formulated by author Napoleon Hill in his bestselling book *Think And Grow Rich* (1937). In the book, Hill defined the Mastermind principle as, "The coordination of knowledge and effort of two or more people, who work toward a definite purpose, in the spirit of harmony." According to Hill's principle, the so-called "mastermind" is not any particular individual but rather the collective intelligence of the whole group. Hill points out in his book that "No two minds ever come together without thereby creating a third, invisible intangible force, which may be likened to a third mind." This "third mind" is the "Mastermind."

In recent years, Mastermind groups have been growing in popularity as a powerful way to accelerate success in people's personal and professional lives. Mastermind groups are a practical application of what is known as "collective intelligence." *Collective intelligence* is a shared or group intelligence that emerges from the collaboration and communication between individuals in groups and teams.

This phenomenon is not always easy to produce in a group. There are many examples of groups that do not display any increase of intelligence through the interactions of their individual members, but actually the opposite. Mobs and dysfunctional teams and families are examples of this. Collective intelligence requires open communication, mutual trust and respect, curiosity and the commitment to a common purpose.

Thus, creating and facilitating a Mastermind Group is both a rewarding and potentially challenging process. It requires special knowledge and skill. A Mastermind Group is something quite distinct from a class, a coaching group or a networking group.

As an example of the masterminding process and its potential benefits, I began facilitating my own first Mastermind Group in the Silicon Valley in 2013, supported by my colleagues Mitchell and Olga Stevko. Titled *The Successful Genius Mastermind Group*, it was intended to be a year-long program for leaders from different industries committed to exponential growth for themselves and for their businesses. The structure included three live mastermind trainings, monthly live webinars, monthly live small groups, and both in person and virtual support from our facilitator team.

The Mastermind Group processes focused on three areas: Success Factor Modeling and implementation of the proven strategies of the world's most successful business leaders, Implementing Genius Strategies of the greatest minds throughout history, and personal transformation strategies using advanced applications of 3rd Generation Neuro-Linguistic Programming. Working together, members shared best practices relating to these strategies and helped one another to creatively and concretely implement them.

As a result, many group members have been able to significantly benefit from their involvement. Author John Gray *(Men are from Mars, Women are from Venus)*, for example, reported, "After the first weekend group meeting, I got such clarity and energy and even inspiration. I finished the book I'd been working on for two years in just 30 days." The experience has been so powerful and positive for group members that the Mastermind group has now extended into its fourth year.

Mastermind Groups Accelerators of Success provides the practical details necessary to assemble and run such a Mastermind Group. The book addresses such key issues as:

- What is a Mastermind Group?
- How do you benefit from being part of a Mastermind?
- How to give a purpose to your Mastermind Group.
- How long does a Mastermind Group last?
- How to build the profile of your ideal participant.
- How to create trust in your Mastermind Group.
- How to manage time in a Mastermind Group.
- How do you facilitate a Mastermind session?
- What happens between sessions?
- What are examples of Mastermind Group processes?
- How to make a Mastermind Group sustainable?
- How to Deal with difficult people and emotions in a Mastermind Group?

Mastermind Groups Accelerators of Success is the fruit of the efforts of 8 exceptional people: Jean-Francois Thiriet, Céline Baysselier, Eric Baudet, Laurent de Rauglaudre, Nadia Grandclement, Catherine Pena, Christophe Genre-Jazelet and Olivier Christol. They co-wrote the book by applying the principles of collective intelligence over more than one year to produce this impressive work.

The seed for this book came during a three-year certification program on Facilitating Collective Intelligence that I conducted in Avignon, France, beginning in 2011 and sponsored by Gilles Roy and *Vision 2021*. The co-authors met during this program and have remained linked by the knowledge that they acquired during the training sessions in Avignon.

If you want to explore and learn how to create an exciting new way to collaborate, learn, grow and succeed, then this book is for you. I am proud and honored to have been an inspiration for such an important and timely work.

Robert Dilts

Co-Founder, Dilts Strategy Group, NLP University and the International Association for Generative Change.

Preliminary Questionnaire

Before you start reading this book, we suggest that you take a few moments to reflect and ask yourself some questions. Your responses will allow you to get more fully involved with this book's subject matter.

What does it mean, for me, "to be a success"?

For me, "being a success" means:_____

_____

_____

According to you, to be successful, one needs to...? What kind of conditions are, according to you, necessary for you to be successful?

To be successful, one needs to... _____

_____

_____

Now, in concrete terms, how would you know you are successful? What kinds of accomplishments would allow you to say "I am successful"?

I would be successful if... _____

_____

_____

How much time would you give yourself to get to that point ?

To get to the point where I would be able to accomplish that, I would need (number of days, months, years)... _____

_____

_____

Take the amount of time you would need and divide it by 2.

That is the amount of time it should take if you decide to participate in a Mastermind group.

You don't believe it? You should take a look, then, to what John Gray, the well-known author of the best-seller *Mars and Venus* series, of which more than 50,000,000 copies have been sold, has said: *"I want to share with you how much I love being part of this Mastermind Group. I got much greater clarity, more energy and inspiration, and I finished the book I'd been working on for two years in only 30 days. Having access to the strategies of the world's greatest geniuses and most successful business leaders enables me to more easily tap into my own highest genius potential. The people in the group are outstanding, and I highly recommend this group!"* [2]

---

2   http://successfulgenius.com/about/

Introduction

"I got there all by myself, Papa! You saw me, didn't you?" My son is five years old and I am always amazed to see how much getting there, "all by himself," matters to him. You might say that for a five years old that's only normal! When he was younger, he used to express this more succinctly by simply saying *"all by myself"* when he wanted me to allow him to "get there" without any help from me. When I heard him exclaim this with so much satisfaction, and with a proud expression, standing straight up, looking like an "i", to the top of his barely 3 and a half feet or so, I realized to what extent our vision of success, even if we are an adult, is always the same as that of a five year old child. We want to "get there..." all on our own. The myth of the self-made woman/man will still be accepted for a great many years to come.

This desire to do things on our own is also expressed in various ways, even when success depends on the assistance of others, and not solely on us. In sports, we always remember the one who scored the goal, but not the one who made the decisive pass, nor the defender who intercepted the ball. Seriously, what is or on whom does collective success depend? No name, no face. No face, no trace.

The myth of the stand-alone hero will continue to exist for a great many years: "I'm a poor, lonesome cowboy who's far from home," and I'm going to get there all on my own. There is the famous proverb that says: "One advances more quickly in life if they do things on their own..." According to this "lone hero" perspective, satisfaction is equal to the suffering endured, and glory, proportional to the number of scars that one has received.

However, even modern myths demonstrate that heroes who get to their destination never do so alone. Solitary heroes always meet allies, as they move along their path, who will help head toward their goal. Just look at Frodo, in the *Lord of Rings* movie who gets all the way to Mordor because of the support of Sam, Pippin, Merry, Legolas, Gandalf, and Aragorn. It can be easy to overlook, for example, that it's Sam, who with his unfailing faith and friendship for Frodo, will take him up to the abyss where the ring will be destroyed when Frodo is no longer able to lift himself. The outside skills of some, and the inner qualities of others are put in service of the hero.

Similarly, Princess Leia in the *Star Wars* **series**, surrounds herself with Luke Skywalker, R2D2, Hans Solo, and Chewbacca to carry out the rebellion. They are carried along, all at the same time, by the same quest, during which all of them acknowledge the contributions of everyone else, and each of them offers what he or she can so it can be put to good use by the group. Without that support, the hero would not be able to get through her ordeal and undertake the next step.

In our view, these mythological tales reflect reality and a deeper process of success that is frequently overlooked.

When we consider the feats of modern "heroes", such as Bill Gates, Elon Musk, Mark Zuckerberg, Richard Branson, and others, who have changed our lives so profoundly because of their inventions, it is easy to forget that they are heroes who reached the top because a group of people supported them in their quest.

Consider Steve Jobs' description of his creative process:

"...So when a good idea comes, you know, part of my job is to move it around, just see what different people think, get people talking about it, argue with people about it, get ideas moving among that group of 100 people, get different people together to explore different aspects of it quietly, and, you know – just explore things.»

Clearly, Steve Jobs understood the benefits of getting the insight of 100 other people. How many of us can get beyond our own opinion or perspective, and then beyond that of two or three people who are closest to us? It has been said that

Steve Jobs

"extraordinary people do ordinary kinds of things that others don't". That doesn't necessarily mean that those things are complicated; they can be as simple as asking for the opinion of several people who are around you that you can trust.

But where does one find these trustworthy multiple perspectives? What kinds of spaces offer, to business leaders (and we are all the leaders when it comes to our own lives) and senior executives, the chance to be on the receiving end of such help? A lot of people will say that the top of the hierarchy is a lonely place to be, especially when you are confronted by huge decisions. Yes, it is easy to feel alone in the business world; to feel that your support system is growing smaller, the quality of your relationships are becoming downgraded, and that very few have the chance to have a supportive executive board at their disposal.

And even if you are part of a group or a team, the question arises: "**Are spaces where there is enough of a feeling of trust between members offered so that all members can be on the receiving end of those multiple perspectives? It is not just a matter of being surrounded by just anybody but of being "well-surrounded."** The quality of the people in our circle, and the quality of our relationships with them is a greater determining factor, when it comes to group effectiveness than just the number of people in the group. In many companies, senior executives, owing to their hierarchical relationship with their teams, are not able to take advantage of invaluable opportunities for receiving non-distorted, uncompromising feedback.

The description "well-surrounded" also brings up the question: "The people who surround some senior executive, are they the right ones to be around them?" Some top managers overcome their solitary position by calling on consultants. In spite of all the good qualities that consultants might have, they are really generally removed from the daily reality of that manager and can only offer one point of view about the situation that she/he is going through. When everything is changing very quickly, the stakes, for the executive become higher, and her/his need to learn things becomes essential. Nowadays, it is obvious that when you are attempting to accomplish something without any support, just reading a book isn't going to help. (How many of us buy a book and don't read it all the way through, or don't apply what's in it until we get to the end?) Just attending a seminar doesn't work, either. Training only gives you general answers. Without ongoing input and support so we can undertake some new action, we are likely to just keep repeating what we have already done, even if it no longer works.

In order to succeed and progress in today's world, we need to learn quickly, find shortcuts, save time, and effectively model our successes and those of others. Who would be a better team member to advise and support you as a leader or top manager than another executive, who has gone through that same kinds of situations, and whose issues are the same?

"A large group of peers can be better for solving a problem than a small group of experts..."

- James Surowiecki

Furthermore, success is not just a matter of learning quickly. Success requires achieving rapid results with what one has learned. We must not only learn but also transform that learning into action quickly. This leads us to the following question, **"What are the key areas where we need to learn quickly, in an ongoing manner, and which also require us to transform our learning into action, and those actions into results for our business?"**, An effective group of peers helps us to move from simply "knowing what to do" to "doing it." As a result of new knowledge and encouragement from others, we gain the courage to move out of our comfort zone and to take action. This is one of the greatest benefits that comes from participation in a Mastermind group.

The question we seek to answer in this book is "What if there was a way to move forward more quickly and effectively by generatively collaborating with others? **What if there were a path along which you could avoid pitfalls because others who have already gone through it and who could share the results of their experience, and lend you their support?** What if there was a place where ideas could proliferate, which could be a super-catalyst for learning, and which would really speed up results? That would, of course, be a method that runs counter to the principle of the lone hero who succeeds on her or his own.

We believe that such a path and process exists: It is called a *Mastermind* group. Our intention, in writing this book, is to share, with you, our experience in working with this kind of group and the powerful results it can bring, primarily because it makes use of the principles of collective intelligence. The Mastermind group is a pertinent, powerful answer for the challenges that face today's business leaders, executives and entrepreneurs. A Mastermind group is the type of team that people have always fantasized about—it is a real Dream T.E.A.M. (Together Each Achieves More). It may be true that one does advance more quickly when one does things on their own, but we go much farther when we have an effective group supporting us.

Does this seem too good to be true? People who have not yet experienced the power of a Mastermind group may think it is to good to be true. For the record, Napoleon Hill, who invented the term "Mastermind Alliance," and whom we will talk about later, went so far as to say, *"a Mastermind group allows one to accomplish in a year what one would otherwise not be able to accomplish during an entire lifetime".*

The aim of this book is to share with you the conditions that are necessary for leading those who participate in a Mastermind group to the point where they can achieve a very high level of success. We will be covering different ways of bringing people together so that they contribute to a "collective intelligence" and create a "generative collaboration." We will show how intelligence that is already in place can become multiplied and produce results beyond what any of the group members could imagine. That is the promise of a Mastermind group.

> *"Under the right circumstances, groups are remarkably intelligent."*
>
> - James Surowiecki

These groups require specific processes in order to achieve that goal. That is why we want to contribute, through the writing of this book, to the development of Collective Intelligence based Mastermind groups in the world. So we would like to share our experience with you, and allow you, at the same time, to get to know what a Mastermind group is, so you can create your own.

Who should read this book?

The notion of a Mastermind group as a format for personal and collective development is new to most people. When we talk about it to our friends and colleagues, we quickly pick up on the fact that they don't know what it is we are referring to. A lot of the time, people even ask us if we are talking about one of the well-known deduction games, with a joking expression on their faces. No, we are talking about a professional and personal development format for business leaders, senior executives and entrepreneurs. Not everyone is ready or able participate in a Mastermind group. There are important personal characteristics that one must have to be an effective collaborator in a Mastermind group AND to promote good group dynamics.

A Mastermind group is meant for all individuals who think of themselves as entrepreneurs. At first glance, they would therefore seem mainly to be people who are owners of their own businesses, directors of companies, or opinion leaders. It matters little if those companies are giants in the stock market or single-person enterprises: The Mastermind group is meant for individuals who want to develop their business or accelerate their economic model rapidly, no matter what sector they are engaged in, or how much profit they take in.

To be "enterprising" does not just mean that one is the head of a business. Some Mastermind groups are made up of individuals who are not official leaders, or not yet leaders. The group may be made up of students or people in the non-profit sector who have a project that they want to carry out quickly and well. A Mastermind group might also be made up of people who are still searching for a career.

At this point, we should mention some of the personality traits that are needed before one can join a Mastermind group.

* The participant must agree to go along with the principle of learning through contact with others, that is to say, learn from the experience of others. People who think they know better than the rest have no place in this kind of group; that kind of participation will upset the way it is supposed to function. It is necessary for a Mastermindian to be able to have some humility and step back, as much as necessary, and absorb what is going on. She/He doesn't know everything, and she/he, rightly so, wants to benefit from different ideas, resources, and contributions from other members, so that she/he can make some progress.

* She/He needs to be responsible for everything she/he does, and for her/his own thoughts. She/He does not shift responsibility for difficult situations onto others or blame it on the context.

* She/He demands a lot of herself/himself. She/He doesn't take the attitude that she/he has shown up just to have a good time but wants to quickly move forward with her/his project.

* Finally, a Mastermindian truly intends to be successful. Anyone who just pretends that she/he is taking action will only slow down the group's dynamics, and that will weaken the efforts of the rest of the participants.

Sometimes people ask if the Mastermind format is appropriate for business development, similar to a professional co-development group. Our experience is that the Mastermind group is not really a managerial development tool like a co-development group. A Mastermind group is business-oriented more in the sense of "I am developing my own business". So we tend to discourage its use for managerial development purposes.

Nevertheless, some organizations and businesses have developed, as part of their structure, venues that allow their people to take on intrapreneurial efforts. Intrapreneurship consists of an opportunity, given by the organization, to certain employees, to come up with business projects that can be developed for the benefit of the organization (where the project manager is a stakeholder), and it sometimes even allows the intrapreneur to create her or his own business. Google, in particular, practices that form of intrapreneurship. In this latter case of intrapreneurship, the Mastermind format can be successfully used at the level of enterprises.

So this book is targeted, on one hand, at consultants and coaches who wish to better understand the principles, methods and the crucial steps that are involved in facilitating Mastermind groups, before implementing them for clients. On the other, this book is also for people who feel they are entrepreneurs and want to understand how a Mastermind group works, so they can decide if they would like to join such a group.

How to Read this Book?

Most of us are interested in having a precise idea about the specific attributes of a Mastermind group, where collective intelligence is employed. That is why we advise you to start with Chapter 1 before moving on to the rest of the book. That is how you will be able to understand the fundamental characteristics of Mastermind groups, and how they position and differentiate themselves, in relation to other forms of support like co-development, team coaching, and training.

We then advise that you read, after that, Chapter 2 if you are interested in the role of facilitator for a Mastermind group. Do you have all the necessary qualities to start off on such an undertaking? Chapter 2 answers the following question: "Who is the group leader, and what skills should be expected of her/ him?"

Chapters 3 and 4 delve directly into the experience and the rolling out of Mastermind sessions: Once underway, you'll learn about the famous Mastermind "hot seat." But that's not all. We also share some of our techniques in those sections, tools for different activities, as well as thoughts about the dynamics and structure of Mastermind groups.

Chapter 5 is important since it addresses the issue of participants. If there are no participants, then, of course, there is no Mastermind group. You will learn how to find and recruit them, how to dispel apprehensions and doubts from their minds as they are confronted by this new approach, and even how reject candidates who would not be on the same wavelength with the rest of your group. All that is indispensable before you can move forward.

And finally, in Chapter 6, we will present the factors that lead to a Mastermind group's success through time, so that participants' sustained success can be guaranteed.

We should point out that the co-authors of this book are in fact members of the same Mastermind group. We wrote this book using collective intelligence as the starting point; we suggest that you take it upon yourself to find out about it. Each chapter was written by one of us and presents an aspect of the Mastermind group that reflects the experience of its author. You will, at times, pick up on some repetitions, and perhaps even some contradictions, which is indicative of the Mastermind group's eclectic system. At the time of our interviews, which addressed Mastermind groups, an American facilitator spontaneously responded, to the following question, "What makes your Mastermind group different?" "That would be me, because I'm the one who facilitates it."

Individual facilitators will exercise a great deal of leeway when it comes to creating a Mastermind group, since she/he does so based on her/his own goals.

In conclusion, here are some definitions that will allow you to better understand what we are talking about when we describe Mastermind groups:

* **Mastermindian (or Masterminder):** Someone who participates in a Mastermind group.

* **Co-Mastermindian (or Co-Masterminder):** We will use this term to refer to Mastermindians, when they help another Mastermind participant during group processes.

* **Going onto the hot seat, or being on the hot seat:** Going onto the hot seat, or being on the hot seat, refers to the scenario where one Mastermindian asks other Mastermindians to give her/him advice, their opinions, share feelings and highly-developed ideas, unique feedback, so she/he can get beyond an obstacle, develop leadership skills, or improve on a project or business plan. One can use other terms, such as go under the cameras, straddle a rocket, get up on stage, or pick up microphone. The hot seat session can be carried out in a variety of ways. We are going to present some of those in this book (in particular, the "booster").

* **Leader:** She/He is the person who organizes the meetings and manages the processes. In some cases, the group is self-organizing; but in the great majority of cases, a leader is in charge of all the tasks that have to do with organized activities.

* **Facilitator :** We will use the term "facilitator" to designate a leader who has specific knowledge and skills in team dynamics, which she/he uses to lead a group, and more specifically, when it comes to supporting the development of collective intelligence. Generally speaking, she/he is referred to as a collective coach, or a consultant who has been trained in collective dynamics.

Chapter 1

What is the Driving force behind a Mastermind Group?

1.1 What is a Mastermind group?

"Show me your friends and I'll show you your future."

- John Wooden

Napoleon Hill is credited with coming up with the "Mastermind Alliance" concept. In his work *Think and Grow Rich*[1], published in 1937 (and which we recommend to anyone who has an interest in achieving success), Hill describes the main principles that contribute to achieving sustainable success. Based on interviews he conducted with 500 of the most successful people of his time, Hill synthesized the principles that guided them along the path to success. What emerged from these interviews is that people who are successful have the following traits in common:

---

1   Hill, Napoleon, *Think and Grow Rich*, 2016, Official Publication of the Napoleon Hill Foundation, Sound Wisdom.

* a clear, obvious desire for success

* self-confidence

* expertise in some area

* an imaginative mind

* the ability to make decisions

* the ability to plan things out

* perseverance

You will discover as you read this book that a Mastermind group develops most of those attributes simultaneously. Because of their involvement in their Mastermind group, participants get to the point where they:

* have a better idea about what they want (a clear desire for success)

* increase their confidence when it comes to their ability to accomplish that (self- confidence)

* develop their skills to get to that point (engaging multiple areas of expertise)

* free their imagination so they can envisage more possibilities

* become engaged and then make decisions

* facilitate the undertaking of action (planning)

* learn from their failures as well as their successes (perseverance)

The Mastermind group concept appears for the first time in Chapter 10 of *Think and Grow Rich*. For Napoleon Hill, one has to imbue the desire to succeed with more power for it to find expression in the world. He defines power as "organized knowledge" and enunciates three ways that it can be obtained:

* through creativity

* through collective experience (which is also included in books)

* through studies and research

In spite of all our efforts, none of us is ever able to accumulate enough knowledge over the period of a lifetime. No one can be fully creative, have enough collective experience, accumulate enough experience, or do enough research on her/his own. To put it another way, even if we do our best with the knowledge we already have, our knowledge is limited anyway. That which has led us to the point where we are will, in all likelihood, not take us any further if we only rely on ourselves.

Think and Grow Rich is the first book that addresses the Mastermind concept in an overt way; it even talks about the "Mastermind Alliance". On the other hand, it seems that Mastermind groups were started long before our own era. People talk about how King Solomon, already in his time, became wise because of the people who surrounded him. People also talk about King Arthur and his Knights of the Round Table, and even of Benjamin Franklin and his "Junto" group, with whose helped he started the first libraries and fire brigades in the United States. Thomas Edison himself, belonged, between 1915 and 1924, to the Mastermind group known as "The Vagabonds", along with Henry Ford, John Burroughs, and Harvey Firestone. For the record, Thomas Edison only received three months of instruction during his life and relied entirely on others in order to come up with his inventions. It has been said that on the day Thomas Edison's laboratory burned down, Henry Ford showed up with a check for $75,000 and told him to "start over". People also talk about Franklin Roosevelt and his "Brain Trust", which was a group of advisers who were chosen for the different knowledge and skills they offered.

To use a metaphor: perhaps you are familiar with the game in which someone hands out an envelope filled with puzzle pieces to seven or eight people who are told to put the puzzle back together. At the end of the allotted time, the facilitator asks who has been able to do it. Obviously, no one raises their hand. Because what each one of them does not know is that some of them have some of the pieces of somebody else's puzzle. So for each of them to succeed in completing her/his puzzle, she/he needs to get together with the others and collaborate on the task.

So What is a "Mastermind Group" Exactly?

Napoleon Hill defines what happens in a Mastermind group as *"the coordination of the knowledge and efforts of two or several people who work for a common goal, in the spirit of harmony."* For him, "two minds cannot work together without creating a third invisible, intangible force, which is something akin to a third mind." This is where collective intelligence concepts come into play as part of already existing Mastermind models, and make a difference, which is something we will discuss later.

Here are some other definitions for a "Mastermind group," which we came up within interviews we carried out with facilitators and participants in Mastermind groups :

"To be in a Mastermind group means that you are surrounded by exceptional people and that you end up doing some really awesome things."

"A Mastermind group is made up of people who get together to help one another accomplish what they want to most in life."

"It is a group that offers three, four, five, six, or seven pairs of eyes so that my situation can be looked at from different perspectives."

"In contrast to training that offers a specific format, or training that responds to needs related to business management performed by senior executives, which is carried out through interventions from people outside of their companies or organizations, the Mastermind group answers the needs of individual participants by surrounding them with people who are working in the same kind of environment that they are."

"A Mastermind group essentially involves contributing to the success of others, at the same time that we find our own solutions, while it acts to bring us closer to the achievement of our goals and dreams."

"A Mastermind group is a source of encouragement, stimulating ideas, and constructive feedback."

"A Mastermind group is a venue where, although encouragement takes place, what goes on is not necessarily pleasant."

"A Mastermind group is a commitment to share the best of ourselves—our experience, skills, and what we have learned."

"A Mastermind group is a group of wise people, or to put it a little differently, a circle of wisdom."

"A Mastermind group consists of a formal, structured encounter that is focused on a goal that is normally carried out in a non-competitive environment."

"A Mastermind group brings together brilliant, enthusiastic, motivated people, under optimal conditions."

Here is what some who have written about them have to say:

"A Mastermind group is a group of talented, motivated people, each of whom has a different background and a different way of thinking about things, but which is concentrated on unleashing the organization's potential[2]."

"A Mastermind group is a practical method through which you can take ownership of yourself and benefit, on the basis of the experience, training, education, expertise, and intelligence of others, as if all that is your own[3]."

"Mastermind groups combine things like brainstorming, training, the taking responsibility for peers and support groups, with the goal of strengthening your business activities and personal skills[4]."

"A Mastermind group is a place where you can share your challenges and ask for help in a constructive way, that is to say, for a guided solution[5]"

And finally, here's the definition we propose: **"A Mastermind group is one that includes entrepreneurial people in search of excellence and the rapid development of their businesses, and is, in general, led by a facilitator who is experienced in the logic of collective intelligence."**

---

2   Dias, Carlos, *Creative Leadership for Turbulent Times, in Collaboration with Jay Abraham*, online program: www.creativeleadership.info.

3   Hill, Napoleon, in (Hill, N., Stone, W. Clement, (1960), *From Success through Positive Mental Attitude*, 1960, Prentice-Hall Inc. Edition).

4   Robert Dilts (Formation "Facilitateur en Intelligence Collective, Formation Evolution et Synergie", 2015, Avignon, training document).

5   *The Cloud 9 Mastermind, The Magic of the Mastermind* e-book, www.cloudnineMastermind.

Your Mastermind Group's Vision:
Putting it into Practice

One of the first steps that should be taken to get your Mastermind group going consists of writing about its vision; and that vision answers the question: "What would you like to see happen in this group?"

Here are some simple examples:

"It should be a really great place where the people can be deeply inspired to become what they are best at."

"It should offer a reassuring, positive venue where one can learn, grow, and find greater personal and professional freedom."

We have found that the following formula to be a useful way to facilitate your Mastermind group to define their vision:

"Our group is … (who)_____

which does (what) …_____

for… _____

so that… _____"

A good example of applying this formula is the *Core Leadership Circle's* vision[6]:

"The Core Leadership Circle" is a powerful group of peers that brings business leaders and influencers together on a monthly basis, so they can support and inspire one another, at the same time that they enjoy themselves as they completely accomplish their major goals.

---

6   http://corelc.org

1.2 What is a Mastermind group that employs collective intelligence?

"It is from the clash of two improbable ideas that great ideas are always born."

— Tim Brown, CEO of IDEO

Collective intelligence *is a term that refers to the cognitive abilities of a community, which results from multiple interactions between its members[7]."* It is intelligence, in the greater sense of the term, strongly correlated with the capacity for coming up with new solutions, without needing to reuse existing solutions. Collective intelligence is also strongly linked with the capacity of a community of individuals for adapting to new situations and new problems without relying on past solutions.

Collective intelligence can potentially be used under a number of circumstances. A well-known experiment illustrates this idea[8]: A group of people is shown a transparent container filled with candy and then asked to independently guess how many pieces of candy are inside it (without allowing them to open it). Even if no one comes up with the exact number of pieces of candy, the average of all the answers inevitably comes close to the actual number (within a few pieces). Google employs this principle to determine, in advance, the number of potential users for their product. Similarly, Microsoft applies it to identify the best date to come out with its software.

The behavior of animals provides many examples of collective intelligence such as dolphins that swim at great speed and cross alongside one another, without ever colliding, or birds that fly in swarms without needing to communicate, and schools of fish that regroup to form, in a collective way, a darker, bigger mass, so they can scare off predators.

---

7   https://fr.wikipedia.org/wiki/intelligence_collective

8   Treynor, Jack, Jelly Bean Experiment. http://wisdomofcrowds.blogspot.fr/2009/12/jelly-bean-experiment.html

Studies by Professor Thomas Malone,[9] founder of MIT's Center for Collective Intelligence, came up with the main factors that contribute to the emergence of collective intelligence in groups of humans.

They are:

1. The balanced participation of each person in a group

2. The number of women in the group.

3. The ability of each member to recognize and respond to the emotions of the other members in the group. (This criterion has a high positive correlation with the preceding one, since women often tend to understand emotions better than men.)

This last criterion is fundamental to collective intelligence. In other words, emotional and social intelligence are key factors when it comes to successfully creating collective intelligence.

This brings us to one of the fundamental guidelines for facilitating Mastermind groups, specifically, that of using the principle of multiple intelligences.

Rather than just operating from cognitive intelligence and a purely-thinking mind, a Mastermind group that makes use of collective intelligence engages four other essential capacities:

* emotional intelligence;

* somatic intelligence;

* relational and systemic intelligence;

* "meta intelligence"; i.e., the capacity to include all of these different kinds of intelligences inside the Mastermind group's space-time container.

Cognitive intelligence is symbolically represented by our brain, emotional intelligence, by our heart, and somatic intelligence by the intestines (enteric nervous system). In fact, modern neuroscience has shown that there are highly complex systems of neurons and synapses in the heart and intestines. (The nervous system surrounding our intestines, for instance, is equivalent to the brain of a cat).These discoveries confirm the age-old hunch that there is an "intelligence of the heart" and a "gut intelligence".

---

9   http://cci.mit.edu/malone/index.html

A major part of facilitating collective intelligence in a Mastermind group involves calling upon all four kinds of intelligence in each individual, as well as at the group level. This includes applying them to define the goal the group wants to accomplish. This is very significant, especially when it comes to the recruitment of members for your Mastermind group. For example, we have found that many effective Mastermind groups seek out people who demonstrate intelligence of the heart even more than their business successes or the length of time they have been in their profession. One might even say that Mastermind groups are "brain", "heart", or "gut" oriented. The Mastermind collective intelligence approach calls on all of those capacities at the same time.

> *"The quality of results produced by any system depends on the quality of awareness from which people in the system operate."*
> — Otto Scharmer

Participants in a Generative State

When multiple intellects become activate, and it's the facilitator's task to ensure that, the group is able to experience what is called a generative state. It is a state where each one of the members is deeply in touch with herself/himself, and, at the same time, something greater than herself/himself. This state brings about, for a group, creative results that are beyond the competencies of each individual member, just like the things that a hand, taken as a whole, can do are greater than what a single finger can do, on its own.

Have you ever participated in a group where ideas seem to emerge by passing through you, rather than coming from your own mind? These frequently come as original ideas, charged with emotion. It's difficult to forget such moments, when group members experience a generative state. It is also easy to notice when group members are not in a generative state. The group goes limp. People become bored. They get the impression that they are wasting their time and energy… On the other hand, when the group is in a generative state, all of the different kinds of intelligence (body, heart, brain, mind), work at 200 %, at the same time and in the same place. The group is then functioning at full throttle, elevating all of its members. And that's nothing less than exhilarating!

> *If you don't allow the harmony that's supposed to be present in your Mastermind alliance to mature, that isn't a Mastermind group. That's just a certain level of cooperation, or some coordinated effort.*
> – Andrew Carnegie

The Generative Field

When a group engages in generative collaboration, the process begins to spread beyond the group; it starts to take place all around the group and with others. Ideas bounce off of one person and onto another, gain momentum, converge, and everyone learns because of three simultaneous phenomena that the generative state produces:

1. **The Phenomenon of Resonance** refers to our nervous system's, or more specifically, our "mirror neurons'" ability to pick up on emotions and the motives behind other's behaviors. This ability of everybody in the group to fall in step with the others brings about an "uplifting effect" that makes everyone feel as if their hearts are beating as one. It is not uncommon to hear the following type of comment in a Mastermind group: "It's unbelievable what (she/he) has shared with us. It's as if (she/he) was directing her/his words directly to me. Even if (she/he) was not addressing me directly, what was said was completely applicable to my own situation". This is a concrete expression of what would be called "resonance." Resonance results from the question: **"What connects us?"**

2. **The Phenomenon of Synergy** refers to the ability to see our differences as things that complement each other and, in that way, produce generativity. This ability is illustrated by a quote from Thomas Jefferson: "If two people swap a dollar, each of them has one dollar. But if two people exchange an idea, each of them then has at least two ideas." Synergy comes from exploring the question: **"What are the differences that we have that enrich each other?"**

3. **The Phenomenon of Emergence** refers to the ability of one system to produce other systems that become more and more complex, and more and more extensive, because of the multiplicity and quality of members' interactions. This is similar to when hydrogen and oxygen molecules mix to produce water, which is a system, itself, that transcends its original components. The relevant question here is: **"What new can emerge through the way we resonate, and from our synergies?"**

These three phenomena make the generative state possible, at the same time they reinforce it.

Together, these three phenomena will contribute to the creation of what we call a collective intelligence **"field"** in the group; that is to say, **"a kind of space or energy created by relationships and interactions between individuals who are part of the same system."**[10]

It is through the interaction between Mastermind group members that collective intelligence emerges. This is what makes Mastermind groups so unique. One of the primary goals of a Mastermind group is to create interactions that generate a collective intelligence field. The quality of this field is also the reason why participants will want to keep returning to the group every month, year after year. It is the facilitators responsibility to maintain this high quality of interaction.

Participants join a Mastermind group in order to experience the benefits of this field. They want to create a collective field in a conscious way. Some call it a "state of flow", which is the highest state one can reach while they are in a group. The participants in a Mastermind group that takes advantage of the principles of collective intelligence look to the facilitator to support the creation of this generative connection. It's the same thing as "team" or "group spirit". And the generative capacity of a Mastermind group greatly depends on the quality of this field. The creation of the field is the first and most important goals for Mastermind groups. The quality of this field needs to be high so that participants in the Mastermind group will have the desire to come back to each and every session.

For the facilitator, to lead a Mastermind group, using the principles of collective intelligence, means that she or he is capable of creating the conditions for a harmonious and generative experience. Without the factor of harmony, even a mutually beneficial association is nothing more than just ordinary or friendly cooperation. The facilitator, herself/himself, is an important actor when it comes to the quality of relationships in the group; and the success of its facilitation depends, to a very great degree, on her or his inner state.

> *"The success of an intervention depends on the inner condition of the intervenor."*
>
> – Otto Scharmer

---

10   Dilts, R., Delozier, J., Bacon Dilts, D., NLPII, *The Next Generation* (2010), p. 243, Metapublications.

In a Mastermind Group: Beware of groupthink!

The opposite of collective intelligence is known as "groupthink", which is defined as "a method of thinking that people use when they are deeply involved in a united group, where the desire to get along exceeds the motivation to come up with other solutions in a realistic way"[11]. Great care should be taken so that this phenomenon does not surface in Mastermind groups. If it does, it will greatly increase diminish the group's added value and the members' return on their investment.

1.3 What a Mastermind Group Is Not

It is important to keep in mind that the primary purpose of a Mastermind group is not to offer support for a team or group as a whole, but rather to provide individual support within of the framework of a group. In this sense, a mastermind group differs from a therapy group, collective training, group coaching and co-development groups. A helpful way of understanding the differences is to look at the various ways such groups operate.

A particular group's support can be centered on:

* **Eliminating a problem or searching for a new solution.** The "pathogenic" version of this focuses on eliminating suffering, while the "salutogenic" approach focuses on achieving optimal functioning and total wellness. Although these two orientations are different, they are not mutually exclusive.

* **Action or reflection.** The group's support may be directed more towards spoken language and reflection (i.e., more symbolic), or towards action and example (i.e., more operational in nature).

* **Lifestyle stability or change.** Support can be aimed at improving things within the context of the person's current style of life. Alternatively, it could be focused on helping her/him go where she/he wants to even if it means changing everything?

* **Content or relationships.** The group's support could emphasize the acquisition of new knowledge or skills, or it could instead be centered on the quality of the person's relationship to hem/herself, among people, or the group's dynamics?

* **Identity building or behavioral reinforcement.** Support can be targeted at reinforcing individuals' behaviors, through the use of techniques and tools, or at enhancing their personal and/or professional identity?

---

11   https://fr.wikipedia.org/wiki/Pensée_de_groupe#cite_ref-1

It is instructive to look at which of these various types of modalities are applied by different types of groups; i.e.,: talk groups (for therapeutic purposes), training groups, collective coaching and professional co-development groups. Consider the table below. For each type of group, indicate whether you think they are centered on a problem and/or solution, action and/or reflection, lifestyle stability and/or lifestyle dynamics, content and/or relationships, or identity building and/or new behaviors.

Group centered on	Talk therapy	Collective training	Group coaching	Co-develop-ment	Mastermind
Problem					
Solution					
Action					
Reflection					
Stability					
Dynamics					
Content					
Relationships					
Identity Building					
Technical Contributions					

The following responses show how we look at all of this. Are our opinions the same as yours?

Group centered on	Talk therapy	Collective training	Group coaching	Co-develop-ment	Mastermind
Problem	Yes	Yes	Yes	Yes	Yes
Solution	No	Yes	Yes	Yes	Yes
Action	No	Yes & No	Yes	Yes	Yes
Reflection	Yes	Yes	Yes	Yes	Yes
Stability	Yes	Yes	Yes	Yes	Yes
Dynamics	No	Yes	Yes	Yes	Yes
Content	No	Yes	No	Yes	Yes
Relationships	Yes	Yes & No	Yes	Yes	Yes
Identity Building	Yes	No	No	Yes	Yes
Technical Contributions	Yes & No	Yes	No	Yes	Yes

We are not, of course, trying to criticize these different approaches, at the same time that we praise Mastermind groups, but are instead trying to point out what makes Mastermind groups unique. This matrix is very important in order to understand the facilitator's role, as well as for the recruiting potential participants. It allows a Mastermind facilitator to ask potential participants about the expectations they have for becoming a member of the group and to establish the proper framework for facilitating the group process.

One of the key benefits of a Mastermind group is that it integrates all of the various methods applied by the other types of groups:

In a Mastermind group, the participants:

* Present their problems and are called upon to research and share solutions.

* Reflect on their situations, and the group calls upon them to act, using those situations as a springboard.

* Work on evolving both their businesses and personal lives. Stability is only thought of as just one phase in the process.

* Benefit, not from theoretical knowledge, but from knowledge that comes from listening to the experiences of other members, and putting things into practice.

* Are surrounded by peers, leaders, senior executives, and entrepreneurial individuals (who are likely a bit more "advanced" than they are in certain areas). This contact reinforces their own identity as leaders, and, as Jim Rohn pointed out: "*We become the average of the five people with whom we spend the most time.*" Our resonance with role models stimulates and strengthens new behavioral expressions and nurtures the natural evolution of our identity.

Let us now take a look at what makes a Mastermind group that employs collective intelligence unique and how it differs from other forms of support. It has to do, in great part, with *responsible, reciprocal engagement.*

We believe that this is the criterion that makes Mastermind groups different from other forms of support groups. Co-development groups also use the principle of responsible engagement, but in a way that is a lot less intense. In co-development, the person who wants to commit herself/himself to taking acting might do that but it is not an obligation. On the other hand, this commitment to take action is a fundamental necessity in a Mastermind group. Since each participant commits herself/himself to particular actions in front of his or her peers, it creates a very powerful network of people who make reciprocal commitments to take action. This commitment, based on feelings of responsibility, is made at the cognitive level, but even more so at the emotional level, and this latter element is what makes the group so powerful.

Once accepted into a Mastermind group, each person commits to taking action, at first, for herself/himself, but also to be of service to the other group members. And there, too, is the difference in relation to co-development: Each person becomes a high-quality resource for all of the others; each one will give her or his "all" to the rest (that does not mean that she/he will do so in the place of the others, because that would leave the latter with no sense of responsibility). Each person commits to doing everything she/he can so that other members are able to get together and achieve their goals, using her or his time, network, and competencies. We will see later that a good facilitator will favor the inclusion, into her or his Mastermind group, of people who seem as if they are going to be as capable of "giving" as they will be of "receiving."

Mastermind groups are also very different from discussion groups. A Mastermind group is strongly oriented towards action, and towards the action-result-feedback loop of events. Every time that a participant presents a situation, asks the group for help and, as a result, is able to gather an abundance of ideas and advice, she/he commits to put them into practice so she/he can improve her/his situation. Frequently, participants come up with a plan of action when they are on the "hot seat". At the time of the next Mastermind meeting, the facilitator will ask them what have has set in motion, about the results that have been achieved, and possibly talk about what is still needed so that participants' actions can be more effective. We'll go more into that later in this book: Suffice it to say for now that *mistakes and failures are better tolerated in a Mastermind group than procrastination and inactivity*.

In summary, here is what we see as a Mastermind group's added value when compared to other forms of support: it compels one to do things because it is confrontational, gives one a sense of responsibility, and exposes one to the consequences of their action or inaction. **Who, nowadays, actually has the opportunity to be confronted in this way, in a caring but non-complacent environment, by such a diverse group of peers?**

Two Testimonies

> *"What makes a Mastermind group unique is what seems like an almost mannerly commitment, on the part of each of the participants, which is supportive of the success of the others in the group. If something happens to one of the group's members, they feel a responsibility to do something to help her/him, well beyond what they would have done for someone with whom they have gone through a training group, for example. There is a real spirit of fraternity in a Mastermind group! You feel very close to the other participants. It's a really good experience."*

"When I was up against some complicated business problems, one of the members of the group got on a plane and went, at his own expense, to spend the weekend and work with my team."

In a Mastermind group, the issue of putting knowledge or skills into action does not need to be brought up, like it is in training groups, since putting what you have received into action is assumed. One of the key conditions for participation in a Mastermind group is that you must apply what you have learned.

To conclude, there are a number of methodologies that are used to involve individuals in order support the goals of a particular group. A Mastermind group takes the reverse approach in that it involves the application of collective intelligence to support the individuals in the group to achieve their personal goals. That is where its originality lies. At the same time, a Mastermind group possesses numerous qualities that are found with most other forms of group process. In fact, it possesses all of them, as is summarized in the following table; and that is what makes this kind of group so powerful.

Group centered on	Talk therapy	Collective training	Group coaching	Co-develop-ment	Mastermind
Generativity	Yes & No	Yes & No	Yes & No	Yes & No	Yes
Emergence	Yes & No	Yes & No	Yes & No	Yes & No	Yes
Resonance	Yes & No	Yes & No	Yes & No	Yes & No	Yes
Synergy	Yes & No	Yes & No	Yes & No	Yes & No	Yes
Fields	Yes & No	Yes & No	Yes & No	Yes & No	Yes

The degree of a group's generativity is a function of the quality of resonance and synergy between participants, and the resulting emergence of a rich and creative relational field. This is what produces the collective intelligence characteristic of a Mastermind group. The creation of this field is the facilitator's main focus. Then there is responsible commitment to action of each group member, as well s the commitment to support all of the other group members to succeed. These are the primary factors that make Mastermind groups different from other forms of collective support groups.

1.4 What are the Basic Premises that Underlie a Mastermind group?

Even though, as we have just determined, a Mastermind group is different from co-development group, their basic premises have a great deal in common. Payette and Champagne[12] have defined a number of principles operating in a co-development group that can also be applied to, and enhanced by, a Mastermind group.

1- **"Practice produces knowledge that science is unable to produce."**
It seems obvious that it is by actually doing something that one learns how to do it. Yet, so many group learning experiences tend to put their primary focus on theories and ideas (as the saying goes, "one should live in theory, because, in theory, everything goes well.") A Mastermind group exploits, to the maximum, learning by experience. This is the focus and responsibility of all the group members.

2- **Learning some professional practice is the same thing as learning how to take action.** The heart of a Mastermind group, its source and expression, consists in encouraging participants to take action, using the new "materials" that they have received during sessions. Participants don't show up to find out more about some particular topic. Rather, they are coming because they want to take action. Learning through taking action is fundamental in a Mastermind group. From that comes commitment to action at every session. If you don't put what you have learned into practice, you deprive the rest of the group of learning. Even if the action you have taken didn't work, you use your mistakes as a starting point. The Mastermind facilitator must also carry out her/his role of coach through a focus on action: making sure participants are clear about where, when, with whom, with what they will take action. She/He also confronts individual members of the group when sessions are not followed by results.

As an example, one of our Mastermind group participants who went on the "hot seat" (or *love seat)* said: "I would like to understand why I never have the courage to say no." The facilitator and other group members quickly reminded the person that the goal of the Mastermind session is not that of understanding "why" but of moving in the direction of the "how". The group led her, in a concrete way, to the identification of what and to whom she would like to say "no", and helped her come up with some concrete strategies for doing that.

3- **Exchanges with others about experiences allow learning which would be impossible otherwise.** A Mastermind group creates supportive exchanges through the practice of structured exchanges between peers. It's not just a simple discussion, conversation, or course. These

12   Payette , A., Champagne, C., *Le groupe de codéveloppement professionnel* (2012), Presse de l'université du Québec.

exchanges, which are organized by the facilitator, guarantee the progress of each participant. Knowledge is constantly evolving or stabilizing. Exchanges with younger peers are a way to keep up to date on things, or you can learn about things that never have changed from those who are older.

4-The participant who takes action is a unique person who is in a unique situation. One of the assumptions in a traditional training group is that it is possible to offer pre-made tools and strategies to participants that can be applied similarly by everyone, regardless of their specific context or personality. This is not the case at all for a Mastermind group. The purpose of a Mastermind group is to offer multiple perspectives and possibilities tailored to the specific situation and unique personality and capabilities of a particular participant. There is no ready-made answer. The group member on the "hot seat" chooses from among all of the ideas that are offered to her/him, selecting those that correspond best to her or his situation.

5-The participants' subjectivity is as important as the objective nature of the situation. In Mastermind groups, the members attempt to understand in what specific way a particular situation poses a problem for the person on the "hot seat" rather than focus only on the objective facts of the situation. In other words, the participants look beyond the situation, such as it is, objectively, to the way the individual is experiencing it. A situation might pose a problem for one individual but not for others. Caring about what the situation poses as a challenge for that person, in particular, allows the group members to come up with answers and solutions that are always more pertinent for person on the "hot seat."

6-Working on professional identity is at the core of effective co-development efforts. Being amongst caring peers is beneficial when it comes to developing one's professional identity. As Jim Rohn asserted, we become the average of the five people with whom we spend most of our time. And that social experience strengthens our identity.

7-Each individual is the expert when it comes to her/his situation and issue. In a Mastermind group it is important to recognize the natural competence of individual participants. The facilitator and the other participants must let go of any feeling of duty when it comes to offering a suggestion to the person who is presenting her/his situation. By coming to a Mastermind group, you are not showing up to affirm your incompetence, but instead to acknowledge your autonomy and the responsibility you have when it comes to finding and applying solutions to the situations that you are confronting. In other words, it's you who knows if a particular suggestion is pertinent, and how to make it pertinent, in relation to your own situation.

8-To learn how to take action, it is necessary to allow some room for personal deficiencies. This principle can be summed up in the following sentence: "We don't always achieve our goal, but we always get some result". And like Nelson Mandela said: "Sometimes I succeed, sometimes I learn." Taking note of our deficiencies is a major resource in that it allows us to learn what we need to. We sometimes meet with failure; that also, paradoxically, brings us closer to our goal. Minimally, you could say that have just found another way how to not solve your problem. We learn from our mistakes as much as from our successes. Each Mastermind group encounter allows participants to learn about what did and did not work, and to identify the "difference that makes the difference."

9-The quality of relationships in a group determines the quality of the content of the exchanges that take place within it. One of the conditions that is necessary for resonance, synergy, and emergence to take place is the quality of the relational field that the group is able to create. A an analogy, each finger on a hand is able to complete a certain number of actions. But when they are all put together, they become a hand that is capable of much more than a single finger can do on its own. That is why the facilitator's support of the creation and maintenance of this field's quality, during work sessions is so fundamental. That's the primary focus of her/his role.

10-The added value in a Mastermind group is directly proportional to the generative state of mind of each member of the group. Not all groups are generative. A group can come together in such a way that the productivity of the group is actually less than it would be if each participant were working on his or her own. In other words, $1 + 1 = -1$. This is common in teams where there are conflicts and tensions, and everyone is trying to sabotage the other person.

In other cases, a group's productivity is essentially the sum of what each participant is able to achieve by working on his or her own. In these two cases, being in a group does not contribute any added value and does not represent any benefit for participants. Because of generative field created between participants in a Mastermind group, the group's productivity is much greater than the sum of its parts; that is, $1 + 1 = 3, 4, 5, 6$, etc.. In short, there is a creative consciousness in an effective Mastermind group – a field that emerges from shared intent, resonance, and synergies between group members.

11-The alignment of a group towards a common intent causes each of its members to converge in the same direction. An effective Mastermind group is one that has a clear orientation. This clarity allows participants to offer one another the most relevant support. This shared intention is an important success factor for an effective Mastermind group. The group's facilitator needs to focus on "recruiting" participants who have similar intentions, and which are in agreement with her/his Mastermind group's main purpose. It is important for the facilitator to emphasize the common intention of group members at the time the group is launched, and whenever a new member is added. The degree to which the group members share a common intention will determine the group's generativity, as well as the quality of each member's results.

The premises listed above are important because they are the foundations upon which a Mastermind group is built. They are the points of reference for the group's conception and facilitation, and for the recruitment of new participants. For example, a fundamental belief, shared by all participants in a Mastermind group, is that one can learn from the experience of others and thereby improve her/his business practices. If you find yourself in front of an individual who says that she/he is interested in your group but only believes in university, scientifically-based learning, that person, will struggle as a member of a Mastermind group.

Expressed in other terms, these 11 principles are the explicit expression of the values on which a Mastermind group operates:

* **Pragmatism**
* **Learning**.
* **Sharing**
* **Trustworthiness**
* **Authenticity/Self-knowledge**
* **Ecosystemic Approach**
* **Autonomy**
* **Creativity/Innovation**

It is important for Mastermind group facilitator to understand these principles well because they call for a particular mindset and require the facilitator to be aligned with those values. They also provide the criteria to be used when recruiting new participants into a Mastermind group. Are the participants pragmatic? Are they trustworthy? Do they have the desire to learn and share, the authenticity, and enough autonomy to actively participate in the group?

In addition to understanding these fundamental premises and vlues, it is important to familiarize yourself with the different types of Mastermind groups. There are a number of key issues to consider when thinking about forming a Mastermind group.

1.5 Different types of Mastermind group

Personal or Professional?

We have said that the group should have a clearly defined goal. And although we have primarily spoken about participants who are business leaders and entrepreneurs, these are not the only people who can make up a Mastermind group.

Conceiving of, being a member of, and facilitating a Mastermind group is essentially a function of applying the principle that a person becomes more intelligent and creative if she/he is supported by a group rather than if she/he is trying to accomplish things on her/his own. Several heads are better than one (generally speaking). This is true both in the case of an individual's personal and professional life. Therefore, you should feel free to create a Mastermind group that addresses both professional and personal concerns. All the principles that we are putting forward apply equally to both situations.

In our study of effective Mastermind groups, we found a facilitator who brought four of her friends together every month, not for an "all-girls party", but for structured discussions. What was their goal? To evolve, professionally speaking, and to find the support and advice they needed. There are also Mastermind groups formed of people who have decided to write a book together, or to help one another find the needed funds to pay for a trip around the world, or individuals who want to share their spiritual development with others.

How Many People Should Be in a Mastermind Group?
Micro and Mega Mastermind Groups

The smallest Mastermind group would be one with two people. One could call it a "micro Mastermind group". We don't think that it is necessary to wait until you have five or six people before you launch a Mastermind. Starting with two is an initial step that is easy to accomplish. Starting with just two, instead of waiting for a third person, shows that those individuals are already quite committed to the spirit of the Mastermind philosophy, which is to act without delay. Napoleon Hill made the observation that a happy marriage is like a Mastermind group because it's a space where each individual is able to become something greater than herself/himself on his/her own.

The difference between a two-person "Mastermind group" and a "discussion between friends" has to do with the framework within which the activities are carried out. In a Mastermind group (even one with only two participants) the facilitator schedules regular meetings in advance, and each member makes a commitment to attend. Participants refrain from "back of the bus" or "sports bar" kinds of discussions. The process is facilitated by one of the members who make up a micro Mastermind group. The goal of the exchanges is to get one to take action. Each person comes to the "group" with a goal she/he wants to achieve and expresses a need and a question. Each member commits to taking action. Each one of them presents her/his reality exactly like it is, and not like what she/he wishes it would be. One person talks, the others listen and offers feedback. Feelings are considered as important as cognitive understanding (we will soon take a look at this important point).

The Value of Micro Mastermind Groups

Significant results can be achieved even in a two-person micro Mastermind group "Nicolas," for instance, is a participant in a micro Mastermind group with a friend that they have titled "taking back your health." As a result, Nicolas has dropped more than 40 pounds by playing sports on a regular basis. Another example is Hervé, who established a micro Mastermind group with another person to improve their public speaking abilities. He and his colleague have become a popular keynote speakers.

Of course, the potential created through a two-member Mastermind group can be increased further by including a third person. When there are just two members, the comfortable feeling of there being just "you and me" settles in. When there is a third person, she/he might turn out to be a third party who contradicts, adds nuances, balances out, and clarifies discussions; therefore, she/he can greatly enrich the generativity of the interaction. This generativity increases exponentially as the group expands to include 5, 6, 7 or more people.

On the other hand, even in Mastermind groups where there is a larger number of participants, we recommend that you create two-person support teams. Two participants who have a lot in common can join together and be co-coaches. Natural affinities between certain individuals in a group will sometimes spark off the creation of these two-person teams which can increase the effectiveness of the larger group. A good facilitator will frequently encourage those kinds of micro Mastermind teams to emerge.

This is especially important for mega Mastermind groups, like that of Jeff Moore[13] in the United States, where there can be as many as 300 participants. It is essential for the effectiveness of the whole group, in such a case, to create sub-groups and micro Mastermind groups.

---

13   https://www.thesuccessalliance.com/jeff-moore-Mastermind-group/

The significance of the Dunbar Number

The Dunbar Number corresponds to the number beyond which a group has a hard time maintaining a strong, stable social bond and good quality relationships. Here is the formula: N X (N – 1)/2. To put it in concrete terms, if you have seven members in your Mastermind group, each person needs to maintain a total of 21 relationships in the group. This level of complexity is just manageable by most people. With just two more participants, that is to say, a total of nine, each person would need to manage 36 relationships. That increase makes it much more difficult to give proper attention to every member and to manage the group. Thus, seven group members seems to be the maximum number for an effective subgroup in terms the quality of the group's concentrated efforts and its interactions.

Participation Ratios

To determine the proper size for a Mastermind group and how often the group should meet, the facilitator needs to figure out her/his group's participation ratio. This calculation allows you to find out if the group offers enough opportunities for the participants to go onto the "hot seat." To find that out, calculate the number of hot seat sessions that will need to take place during the time that your Mastermind group will be in existence. For example, a group that meets ten times a year, and which offers three opportunities to go onto the hot seat per day, offers up to 30 opportunities to be on it over a period of a year. This number should then be divided by the number of participants in any given group so that the number of possible people who are to go onto the hot seat can be ascertained. In this example, if there are 30 total opportunities on the hot seat, in a group of 20 people, there would be 1.5 opportunities, every year for each individual. That's not all that many. If there were 12 Mastermindians in the group, on the other hand, it would amount to 2.5 times per person. With 6 participants, the number would increase to 5 times per person – that is to say, one every two months. Clearly, the higher the participation ratio, the greater the number of opportunities for participants to benefit from the advantages the hot seat has to offer.

A Common or Individual Goal?

We have been emphasizing throughout this book so far just how pertinent it is to have a clearly defined, common goal, at the core of a Mastermind group. This does not mean, however, that all of the participants' profiles should be the same. On the contrary, diversity greatly enriches the collective intelligence of the group. Conversely, a Mastermind group that is made up of participants who have different goals will not survive for very long.

In our experience, there can be three kinds of Mastermind groups that may be equally effective:

1. Those in which the members have similar profiles and share some common goals. For example, a group of friends that decides to read a book together and then apply its principles to their personal lives.

2. Those in which the members have similar profiles and different goals. For example, executives who want to experiments with new governance models for their organization and who show up so they can learn from and help other members to try something new.

3. Those in which the members have different profiles and but share some common goals. For example, those who are in positions of responsibility in different areas (industry, advising, and medicine), and who want to become conscious leaders.

There are also groups that can actually be quite problematic:

* Those in which individual profiles are different, and where there are also different goals. This is more likely to create chaos and should be avoided.

We have observed that it is often the case that similar profiles have frequently determined who has been recruited for participation in a particular Mastermind group. Those participants' goals, however, can still be different. In other words, we have noticed that similar profiles, rather than similar goals are more often used as the organizing criterion for a Mastermind group. That is, you will find Mastermind groups that are made up solely of restauranteurs, senior executives, directors of start-ups, real estate agents, neophyte managers, and even work-at-home mothers. Such Mastermind groups help to reinforce professional and personal identity. When there is too much homogeneity and not enough diversity in these groups, however, there is a marked decrease in their collective intelligence.

Horizontal or Vertical?

The more a Mastermind group is focused on simply handing down a particular person's information and expertise (usually by the group's founder), the more it will just be a vertically-oriented group "supervision", or a Mentoring Mastermind. This approach was illustrated for us during our study of Mastermind groups when, in answer to the question "what is it that makes your Mastermind group different" a Mastermind group founder responded "because, quite simply, I'm the one who facilitates it".

In response to the same question, another Mastermind group founder told us "The Mastermind group that I facilitate is not focused on me but on the participants." We can say that the more focused a group is on mutual support and group dynamics, the more it has to do with horizontally-oriented "intervision".

The concept of *supervision* is an expression of the idea that there is an individual who is in a higher position in relation to the others: She/He is the expert. The individual who has launched the Mastermind initiative of this type often has good answers or a level of success that the other participants have only been fantasizing about. The concept of *intervision* is based on the idea there is no single correct solution to something, and that each group member's map will serve to enrich everybody else's. That is the approach that a Mastermind group which employs collective intelligence offers. Determining the proportion of supervision and that of intervision when designing your Mastermind group is important. It will, in turn, determine the style of facilitation and the type of expectations group members should have.

In our study of various Mastermind groups, we discovered some groups where the facilitators also periodically assumed the role of trainer. They facilitated the Mastermind process in their groups and then added two or three sessions a year that deal with specific themes that surfaced during the Mastermind sessions. These facilitators were, moreover, often chosen for their expertise, such as: Internet marketing, personal appeal, and parenting. Generally, the more famous the facilitator, the more popular her/his Mastermind group will be. While it is entirely possible to offer some training-oriented sessions for a Mastermind group, or to bring in experts or people who share their personal testimonies, it should only take place on an occasional, limited basis. Training-oriented sessions should only be offered because they respond to a specific need of the participants. They should also be done in such a way that they strongly engage group members so that they do not simply become the same as a training session or a seminar.

Mastermind intervision	Mastermind supervision
Circular approach	Pyramidal approach
Rotating interaction between professionals/ facilitator	An expert / a few professionals
All experts	An individual with more advanced knowledge
Focused on the emergence of solutions	Focused on the contribution of solutions
Co-creation of the process and adaptation	Preconceived process
Process-focused facilitator/relationships	Facilitator who is focused on the contribution of content

Differences between Supervision and Intervision

Although we make the assumption that a Mastermind facilitator should be primarily oriented towards intervision, our interviews with various Mastermind groups around the world showed that participants can also benefit a mixture of supervision and some training along with intervision.

Face-to-face or Online Groups

We have already said that Mastermind groups got their start in the United States. given the size of the USA, Mastermind groups frequently require the use of electronic methods for communication. A number of groups will carry out their activities by using Internet technology on a monthly or weekly basis, and then have one or two intense face-to-face sessions per year. In fact, some facilitators only lead online Mastermind groups. Telecommunication methods do offer the advantages of not having to reserve a room or change locations, so the time set aside for the group can be better organized. In addition, participants can be found from a larger geographical area. This can also reduce the risk of competition between members who are local to one another.

If group members are close enough to make it possible, however, we recommend that you employ the face-to-face model. This can be especially important if you are part of a group that gets together only once a month or less. Face-to-face interaction allows the bonds between participants to be strengthened; people become a lot more involved with one another than if they were participating from a distance – in particular, when it comes to the use of the hot seat. For Mastermind groups that are facilitated on a weekly basis, virtual tools for online meetings are a good alternative that allows people to keep up the pace and sustains a high level of focus for participants when it comes to them implementing their plan of action. By creating a very short feedback loop, it helps to promote more intensive individual and collective learning. In any case, we recommend that the initial meeting of a Mastermind group be face-to-face if possible.

Should Participants Pay or Should the Group Be Free?

We will address the cost involved with Mastermind groups in more depth at a later time. For the moment, let's say that the cost of a Mastermind group, to a large degree, depends on the extent of the presence of a professional facilitator. The actual fee people pay will depend on the amount of added value the group offers, which is a result of its organizational and administrative logistics, the amount of facilitation, and the support of the group during the process, for as long as it lasts. The more the members have goals and responsibilities where a lot is at stake, the more frequent the meetings and the more the need to support the group dynamics during and between sessions will be necessary. The more the presence of a professional facilitator is is required to support the group's ambition, the greater the fee. Clearly, there is no pre-established fee for all groups. There are high-end Mastermind groups that can be quite expensive. The cost is even greater when the Mastermind group is based on a supervision model, where an expert brings participants in his Mastermind group together primarily so that they can benefit from her/his expertise. This is frequently the case when a recognized expert attracts people who want to achieve the same level of results that he or she has, in the same professional and personal domain (such as internet marketing, for example). Those are often the Mastermind groups that are the most costly.

Conversely, Mastermind groups that are based on intervision (i.e., the complementary contribution of all the participants) are often less expensive because the responsibility for the group's progress is shared amongst the participants.

A Mastermind group that is fully self-managing is generally free, or may involve a small fee paid at the time of meetings. We interviewed a person who created a Mastermind group on his own, for instance, and the cost for participation was to do nothing more than bring a bottle of something or a dish to be shared during the meeting. The issue of whether a particular Mastermind group should be free or not is a key part of the overall framework of the group and should be addressed from the start.

There are those who feel that all Mastermind groups should be free. We interviewed a person who expressed his regret as soon as he saw that the Mastermind model had turned into one where participants are required to pay a fee. He explained that he saw the groups as a source of support that everyone should have access to. We acknowledge the existence of that point of view, and at the same time, people frequently devalue things that they don't have to pay for. We found inn our own Mastermind group that when it was free for people to participate, it had an impact on the members' degree of commitment and involvement. There were more absences, people were late to sessions, etc. Whatever model you choose, a Mastermind group should not be seen primarily as a source of money, but as a vehicle for building generative relationships and supporting participants.

Here are some tips to consider if you are thinking of starting your own Mastermind:

* Turn your coaching or training clients into Mastermind participants. You have already won their trust, so you will be saving a lot of time!

* Make your experience come to life (on live broadcasts, face-to-face meetings, or during webinars), rather than just talking to people about your group. That is the best way to attract people to your group.

* Keep payment methods simple.

* Have your fee established from the start so that it does not seem so overwhelming.

* Think about your fees: you will either base them on the time that you are actually going to spend on the group every month, multiplied by your hourly fee, divided by the number of participants, or charge a monthly fee, or base your fee on the added value that you think you will bring to the group (a concept often used by Internet gurus).

* Ask for payment in advance and lay out clear rules regarding reimbursement when someone cancels their participation, or when someone is absent from a meeting.

* Make sure that you take the cost of logistics into account— such as interventions carried out by experts, or weekends, when new members are added to the group, or when there is some other kind of celebration—before you decide what the fee should be.

* Finally, you should bear in mind that some participants who get used to not having to pay anything to take part in a Mastermind group will have a lot more problems when they have to do it at a later time. It's better to ask for a minimum fee at the start and make it clear that there will have to be a financial obligation on the part of the participant. We are certain that, once you have made an assessment of everything that is required for the facilitation and preparation for a Mastermind group, you will no longer have any doubt about the need to ask for a reasonable financial contribution.

Can a Person Be a Participant and a Facilitator at the Same Time?

The role adopted by the facilitator should be clear and consistent with the group's structure. In the case of free Mastermind groups, the facilitator could very well be a participant like the others. Some Mastermind groups are even led by rotating facilitators. That can be a really good demonstration of collective intelligence! On the other hand, as soon as the facilitator starts to become paid, we don't recommend that she/he wear the caps of facilitator and participant at the same time. If the facilitator of a Mastermind groups wants to also participate in a Mastermind group, we suggest that she/he join another Mastermind group where she/he will "just" be a participant. As a result, she/he will be more available and productive in both groups. That will allow him/her be able to carry out all the roles that are expected of a facilitator of a Mastermind group more thoroughly.

There are as many kinds of Mastermind groups as there are life situations. Obviously, those that come to mind first are those that are tied in with business issues. There are also special Mastermind groups, however, for single people, couples, the recently divorced, people who want to lose weight, artists, mothers, parents of adolescents, and retired people, too.

The following are some concrete examples of Mastermind groups:

* Friends who meet because they have all read the same book, so they can exchange some ideas about what is in it and talk about how they can apply it to their lives. For example: a Mastermind group that addresses the book, *The Leadership Gold,* by John C. Maxwell[14], and which accompanies the readings of each chapter with exercises.

* Consultants who want to view the video of a seminar or MOOC together. For example: a Mastermind group that studies Otto Scharmer's MOOC U.Lab Theory U.

* Coaches and consultants who want to learn online marketing and blogging. For example: Mastermind groups for online marketing gurus.

* Spouses/heads of enterprises who want to balance their personal and professional lives.

* Businesswomen who are in the first five years of starting their careers.

* Entrepreneurs who have been in business for at least two years and who carry out direct marketing and want to increase their online presence.

---

14   http://lindatravelute.com/leadership-gold-mastermind-group/

Are you familiar with SHUT UP AND WRITE[15] Mastermind groups?

Some people created what has turned out to be an amazing, very clever kind of Mastermind group. Its members meet online for only two hours every two weeks, but they don't talk to one another! Do you know why? Well, because it's a *SHUT UP AND WRITE* group, of course. These groups bring together people who want to write a book and who have never been allowed the time to see such a project all the way through. They then decide to show up regularly at meetings so they are forced to take the time to write with the rest of the members of the group. Yes, they have freely chosen this group just so they can benefit from a forum that requires them to be disciplined. They take advantage of four sequences of writing which are followed by five-minute breaks. Each member's productivity is, as a result, prodigious.

And one shot Mastermind groups?

These groups don't carry out work that lasts over a long period of time. They are created and then broken up, depending on the request of a specific person in relation to a specific issue. Very often, they last only one hour or one day. To put it in concrete terms, a person might have an important issue and want to get some feedback in response to her/his questions and the options she/he has looked at. That person then takes it upon herself/himself to call on and bring together several experts who have experience with her/his issue for a face-to-face meeting or a conference call. The format of the call adheres to the Mastermind meeting process and goes for a predefined period of time. The person organizing the meeting may offer either financial or material compensation for those who take part in it. For example, a few years ago, one American Internet guru found himself in difficulty and had issues that were legal in nature. This was an area that was far removed from the professional domain in which he excelled. He took it upon himself to bring 20 lawyers, who were experts on the problem, in on an hour-long conference call, during which he shared his problem with them. In return for their feedback, he offered, in exchange, an invitation to one of his seminars. He said afterwards that it was probably the best investment he has ever made. He added that none of the lawyers, on her or his own, would have been able to offer him the level of response that he received by bringing together 20 lawyers. Even though not all of us are Internet gurus, we also see, in these kinds of spontaneously created Mastermind groups, a very powerful way of getting instant responses to our issues.

Many Mastermind groups are formed to address specific issues. Group sessions for entrepreneurs may focus on brainstorming how to design a logo, address the creation of passive income, attract new clients, create business cards, share best practices for a website that converts visitors to site into clients, etc. A managers' group may instead focus on issues like dealing with one's boss, establishing goals, managing relationships be-

---

15   https://thesiswhisperer.com/shut-up-and-write/

tween different generations of workers, asking for a raise and so on. Then there are Mastermind groups that address personal development, where the individuals may have an interest, for example, in discovering their true genius, exploring how they can remain positive, finding their passion, managing their fears, or learning how to say "no".

These groups are very different from those that do networking, because the goal of a networking group is essentially that of increasing the number of connections within the group so that it leads to more business opportunities for its members. The purpose of a Mastermind group is to enhance the generative quality of the relationships between the participants. Because of this, most Mastermind groups are of limited size.

1.6 Benefits for Participants

Napoleon Hill introduced the Mastermind group as a venue that allows participants to:

* Find out what they want to find out about in order to reach their desired outcomes and goals.

* Have confidence about their ability to reach their desired outcomes.

* Develop the skills to achieve their goals through multiple kinds of expertise coming from peers.

* Free their imaginations and benefit from the ideas of their group so they can envisage all possibilities and options.

* Make a commitment and make a decision.

* Anchor their decision in action, by planning it out.

* Learn from their successes, as well as their mistakes (and from those of others).

These advantages are important sources of motivation for joining a Mastermind group. We also think that there are some others.

As a part of a Mastermind group, you have an appointment. And it doesn't matter what kind—it can be one that is obligatory, and in the end, one that is freely consented to. Through your commitment to your Mastermind group, you have freely decided to devote time to your professional development, once a month for a year, in most cases. The facilitator will take care of all of the logistics so that your mind will feel at ease from not having to think about all the details. You know that every month you have an important meeting with peers to discuss your business, find solutions, but also, paradoxically, to let your brain refresh itself and recharge your batteries, in good company. And that is already a strong internal process. Several Mastermind group participants say that coming to a meeting is like a recreational activity. There are very few occasions that offer the possibility of being occupied with yourself and your business at the same time.

Since the facilitator takes care of all of the logistics, all participants have to do is to direct their attention to their projects, businesses, themselves, and the quality of their relationships with the other members of the group. All they have to do is free their genius and reap the benefits that come about from exchanges with their peers, thanks to facilitator-led interactions.

The second advantage, and it will seem obvious, is that you are part of a supportive group. Being part of a supportive group can bring benefits that go beyond the cognitive knowledge exchanged by group members. An executive or leader is often alone at the top of the pyramid in her/his organization. And even if she/he has an executive board, the issues that crop up during interactions with professional colleagues can create challenges that can be experienced as paradoxes and become sources of tension.

Some of the challenges that emerge with respect to professional colleagues and team members include:

* Difficulties in assuming a leadership role and at the same time being true to one's personal responses.

* Difficulties in maintaining clarity of vision and proper perspective with respect to a group that is in the same ecosystem.

* Difficulties making objective decisions in an environment where one's status is an important consideration.

The Mastermind group you belong to, on the other hand, is there to support. The members have chosen you as much as you have chosen them. No one is there to shine more than anyone else. Each person comes to it bringing along her/his experience and perspective, her/his strengths and weaknesses, her/his genius, and the areas about which she/he is not clear. Parity reigns. Each individual is basically invited to let her/his mask of a responsible executive or entrepreneur drop away and to, without hesitation, support the one who is looking for help and who aspires to move forward. Otto Scharmer, a professor at MIT, expresses this idea quite well: "Becoming a member of a group of peers is like dropping your knees to the ground and accepting to show your vulnerability."

The third advantage is that you don't have to do anything. What a pleasure it is to know that someone else is taking care of everything:

* Someone organizes everything, often involving places where you would never go by yourself.

* Someone leads the group, using tools that are specific to collective intelligence.

* Someone takes the responsibility to turn exchanges into something that is profitable, so that everyone takes away more than she/he invested in them.

And there is also the possibility that, while you are a member of a Mastermind group, you will allow yourself to be carried away by what is going on, and will not suffer the guilt of allowing yourself to do nothing.

The next to last advantage that we see in relation to your being in a Mastermind group is that **you will benefit from the input of 7, 8, or 9 expert consultants at the same time**: 7, 8, or 9 different professionals, who although they may have different career and life paths and skills than you do will at least be at the same level of success as currently are. They will be there for you, committed to your success (like you will be for them).

So you have 7, 8, or 9 perspectives on your issues, coming from people, without any hidden agendas, who don't work in your field, but who want only one thing—to help you. That is what is at the core of the Mastermind group—those are the "treasures" associated with a Mastermind group. This advantage alone justifies the fee associated with a Mastermind group, and those aren't just empty words! Do the math: 7, 8, 9 coaches, 1 day per month, over the period of 1 year = ...

And finally, the most important advantage, which we share again with you here, is that **a strong commitment exists between members.** Having a meeting set up in advance, that's really good! With a group that has 7, 8, or 9 coaches, that's even better! But a group that appeals to your commitment, that's the best case scenario! It is, for sure, better than engaging face-to-face with yourself. People, as a general rule, love to talk, exchange ideas, think about all of their issues (often by complaining about them), but the Mastermind group is there to make sure that you move on from your dream to implementing the actual project. The group is there to support you through to the very end. It's very demanding and equally very rewarding. And we say this because we have experienced it in each and every one of our Mastermind groups.

The effectiveness of a Mastermind group depends on action-feedback-learning loops. Without action and learning, there can be no progress (or only very little). We learn just as much from our mistakes. When we talk about learning that takes place in a Mastermind group, it has to do with that of the person who is taking action, but also with the shared learning of all the others who are in the group. We share our successes and mistakes. The other group members learn too when they listen to us describe the difficulties we have experienced. Participants are constantly learning from each other through their modeling what works, and what does not work.

Participating in a Mastermind group gives you a good shot of constructive energy. We need energy in addition to knowledge in order to achieve success. Participating in a Mastermind group allows you to generate the amount of energy needed to take a risk and undertake action, come up with innovations, and go even further than that. By the end of each meeting, Mastermind group participants are raring to get to work, fueled by each other's ideas and suggestions, encouragement, and points of view. Participants feel that they are capable of becoming the best version of themselves, and even better than that, because of the example provided by other participants.

As far as we are concerned, there is no doubt that the support provided by Mastermind groups, both today and tomorrow, fulfills a great need for business leaders and entrepreneurs, and of all people who want to succeed in achieving their goals and become more self actualized.

Besides the fact that it is innovative, the Mastermind approach, where collective intelligence is employed, addresses several levels of issues:

* **Identity level issues:** Finding role models and support from other leaders and entrepreneurs.

* **Operational issues:** Finding concrete answers to resolve issues.

* **Financial issues:** Making your business more profitable and innovative.

* **Intrinsic meaning issues:** Taking pleasure in learning and moving forward.

* **Social and emotional issues:** Finding emotional support within the context of learning.

These five can be used as a basis for evaluating the quality of any Mastermind group. Ask your participants to respond to the following statements by using the numbered scale that follows.

Using a scale from 1 to 9, with 1 meaning "not at all", and 9 meaning "definitely", respond to the following statements :

1. Because of my participation in this group, I am becoming, more and more, that which I want to be (identity level support).

        1   2   3   4   5   6   7   8   9

2. Because of my participation in this group, I am able to get concrete answers to my questions (operational level support).

        1   2   3   4   5   6   7   8   9

3. Because of my participation in this group, I am able to make advances in my business (financial level support).

        1   2   3   4   5   6   7   8   9

4. Because of my participation in this group, I find pleasure in learning new things (intrinsic meaning level support).

        1   2   3   4   5   6   7   8   9

5. I derive pleasure from participating in this group (social and emotional support).

        1   2   3   4   5   6   7   8   9

The following is a list of benefits for the Mastermind group participant as an individual:

* She/He is challenged when it comes to her/his ideas and convictions.
* Her/His professional identity is built and strengthened.
* She/He feels that she/he is receiving support.
* She/he has access to greater creativity.
* She/He is forced to think about her/his professional activity in a different way.
* She/He develops self-esteem (without turning into a pretentious person).
* She/He is able to step back and take a look at the whole situation.
* She/He gets a mental workout.
* She/He has access to the other participants' years of experience.

* Her/His level of ambition and/or realism becomes increased.
* Her/His failures are transformed into learning experiences.
* She/He develops her/his capacity for taking action.
* She/He feels more at ease when confronted by uncertainty.
* She/He allows herself/himself to be more authentic (finally!).
* She/He starts to think in new ways.
* She/He feels surrounded and supported by a high quality network of people.
* Her/His relationship needs (to not be by herself/himself) are satisfied.
* She/He learns how to help others.
* She/He learns how to ask for help.
* She/He develops confidence in her/his decisions and acquires a greater capacity for taking them on.
* She/He freely goes along with exercising discipline.
* She/He downplays her/his mistakes.
* She/He has greater self-awareness.
* She/He is able to receive and give encouragement.
* She/He grows up and then grows as a human being.

The following list details some of the benefits for Mastermind group participant an executive or entrepreneur:

* A supportive "executive board" that is devoted to success.
* The ability to immediately model the successes of others.
* Acknowledgment of the actual progress of one's business.
* Easier problem solving. Less attempts at it, and less errors
* Getting multiple perspectives on professional issues.
* New ideas which one otherwise would not have access to.
* Development of strategic and operational maturity.
* Easier identification of the real issues.
* Distance from one's ecosystem (so one can go back into it in a way that is better).
* Acquisition of non-theoretical knowledge, which is based on other participants' experience.

* Acquisition of pertinent, honest (at times, ruthlessly compassionate event !) feedback from people who have already gone through what one is currently going through.

* Acquisition of the ability to move forward more quickly because of other participants' experiences.

* Acquisition of the ability to identity solutions that are outside of one's field of awareness.

* Creation of a network of excellence.

* The experiences, knowledge, information, and skills that one would otherwise never be able to acquire in a single lifetime.

* Being surrounded by co-coaches who promote one's business activities.

* Being challenged, from being forced to go outside of one's comfort zone.

* The refining of one's problem solving skills.

* Accepting one's own vulnerabilities, and turning them into a resource.

* Being decisive and engaging in action.

* Saving time between the stage when one comes up with an idea and the time when one carries it out.

* Taking risks and being daring!

Benefits of Mastermind Groups

Anthony Robbins often shares the story of visiting an army barracks where he had talked to a platoon of soldiers. The general who had invited him acknowledged that the soldiers' experience in the army was one of the most powerful times of his soldiers lives, but went on to lament that most did not make their top-level training an integral part of their lives. As a result, in their civilian lives, they did not have access to success at the same high level they achieved during their time in the army. When Robbins was asked why that was the case, he responded: "When these soldiers leave the army, they no longer have the demands that were imposed on them in that environment, which called on them to do the best they can." Those are the kind of demands that are brought to bear in Mastermind groups.

A Participant's Testimony

"Participating in this Mastermind group has given me self-confidence. And even though we don't see one another every week, it's as if I'm connected to the group and its energy, anyway. It's as if the group were supporting me, even from a distance... I allowed myself to believe that becoming successful would be something that would be accessible to me, and which I would be able to do, too. I then made up my mind to manage my priorities better and to start my day at 10 AM by meditating or doing some sports activity for an hour. I lost about 25 pounds because of that and have increased my energy level. I have now assumed responsibility for being paid the right fee I deserve in my work. And I have made new friends and we often call one another when we are not at the meetings."

Your Mastermind Group's Name

Giving a name to your Mastermind group, when it is well-chosen, reinforces the participants' feeling of belonging. Here is some advice about how to choose one:

* The word "Mastermind" does not necessarily have to appear as part of your name: You can replace it with such words as "circle", "group", "alliance", "community", "collective", etc.

* Choose the name taking into account the kind of people you want to attract: Who are they? What is their age? Who referred them? What are they looking for? What do they have in common? And at the same time, what is unique about them?

* You can choose a title that seems to offer some kind of promise, using verbs that describe what results a person should be able to get: the "Work Less and Earn More Group", or the "We Take Chances Group", to mention a couple of examples.

* You can use words that identify the participants, that is to say, exactly what they want to become: "Mommy Entrepreneurs Group", or "Zentrepreneurs".

* You can also use an image or a sound that is familiar to the participants: "The WOW Group", or even a "All for One Group".

* Your group itself can carry out the activity of finding what would be the right name for itself. That could be an excellent ice breaker at the time of its first few sessions.

Chapter 2

Who Can Create a Mastermind Group?

We are of the opinion that anyone can create a Mastermind group. It is a rather simple thing for one to bring a few of her/his entrepreneurial friends together, so they can, each in her/his own turn, be heard as she/he presents her/his own project, and so that the others can counsel him/her and give their advice. In principle, leading a Mastermind group is not any more complicated than that. Nevertheless, people who create and lead such groups are often coaches or consultants who have experience in the management of groups, and in monitoring collective processes.

For example, the group of eight people who have written this book is only made up of coaches who have undergone training that is specifically targeted at the development of collective intelligence. Such coaches and consultants know how to emphasize the things that are important, the most salient points, and how to make needs emerge, behind the questions, so that the work becomes more effective. They make the creative tension increase when necessary, and regulate the activity that takes place between the participants, but also adopt the correct posture for a leader or facilitator.

In summary, to answer the question "who can create a Mastermind group", our response is everyone, but preferably people experienced in coaching or in the management of small groups.

Whoever decides, one (great) day, to lead or facilitate a Mastermind group will bear the responsibility of carrying out different roles. She/He "recruits" the participants, motivates them, regulates the dynamics of the group, watches to make sure that the members maintain a collective, constructive, and ambitious mindset, leads sessions and interventions, and finally allows the mutual creation of a generative relational field that frees up the genius of each Mastermindian.

2.1 The Mastermind Group Facilitator's Roles

Creation of the Group, and Managing the Group's Human Resources

Recruitment of Participants

Typically, a facilitator will begin by bringing a group of 5 or 6 people together to launch her/his Mastermind group. This is a group size that allows for generative interaction without being too cumbersome to handle.

Enlisting the group members requires a certain amount of promotional work by the facilitator. It is a matter of specific communication skills for which the facilitator may want to enlist help, if she/he feels there is the need. Depending on her/his work habits, communication skills, and the quality of her/his network, the facilitator may recruit from her/his professional network, from individuals to whom she/he is closest (friends, work colleagues, fellow members...), from network events, or by carrying out promotions on the Internet. She/he may choose to do all three.

The facilitator will want to make sure that she/he does not recruit participants whose business activities are too close. This can lead to a risk of the perception of competition between the group members. Furthermore, having participants who all share the same expertise does not provide the necessary level of diversity required to create a rich level of collective intelligence. The facilitator should seek to come up with a Mastermind group that brings together participants who come from very different backgrounds. A wealth of diversity is clearly one of the great benefits of an effective Mastermind group.

Mixed groups, where there are both women and men, are also highly desireable. They guarantee diversity when it comes to the way things are looked at, and allow for the generation of multiple solutions.

At the same time, the facilitator will want to be careful to choose participants who have similar needs. Obviously, the issues that would be pertinent and most relevant for a group made up of unemployed people will be quite different from one whose participants are heads of companies that are listed on the stock market. Some facilitators create their groups based on certain business criteria, for example, that the participant's company has more than $200,000 in annual sales, or more than 10 employees.

The results for a Mastermind group, when it comes to individual or collective success, depend to a very large extent on the "quality" of the group members, which will be a function of their personalities and experiences.

Thus, the facilitator will want to look for certain personality traits in the candidates at the time of the recruitment interview, and in particular, make sure that potential candidates share the values (addressed in Chapter 5) that are part and parcel of Mastermind groups.

This "recruiter" role should be taken seriously, because it is ultimately the facilitator who creates her/his group. She/he is the one who makes the choice about whether or not a certain candidate can become a member of the group. It is not a matter of recruiting a candidate because she/he is a magnate in some industry, or is popular in the press, but of finding out if she/he has the human qualities that will ensure that she/he will be a responsible partner, so that the group's dynamics will be good. The facilitator must have the right to deny the inclusion of certain candidates. This may not be the best for her/his short-term revenue; but it will keep her/him from "shooting herself/himself in the foot."

Besides assessing candidates' personalities, the facilitator will want to make sure that candidates want to commit to attending all of the meetings (in person or online). A commitment to attend is a non-negotiable condition that has to be fulfilled if a person wants to join a Mastermind group. If a candidate is unable to commit to regularly attending the meetings, with almost no exceptions, then she/he should not be invited into the group. When the facilitator recruits "her/his" Mastermindians, she/he should bear in mind that a rejection of a candidate before the group starts is a lot easier, and goes a lot more smoothly, than having to force a participant out later on.

When a facilitator is in the process of signing up a person for her/his Mastermind group, she/he needs to explain just how critical and important the commitment is, what the benefits are for each member of the group, as well as for the participant herself/himself. Regular attendance at the meetings allows the members to get to know one another better as time goes by, and to create connections so that, gradually, teams can be created that will be self-supporting, and which will allow members to help each other out on a day-to-day basis.

The facilitator provides the schedule for sessions in advance and asks the members to set aside the times on their own calendars when they first become registered. If a person is unable to participate on most of the dates that have been set aside for meetings, then she/he, quite simply, is not a good candidate for the group.

Managing Departures from the Group

Creating a group is not limited, of course, to just recruiting and then leading. The facilitator should likewise support the voluntary departure of certain group members. Moreover, if certain members are not sufficiently committed, the facilitator should end their participation. In such a situation, it is imperative that the facilitator communicate, in a factual manner, with the individual in question and the rest of the group, to explain the reasons for the departure. This is a very important move so that the group's cohesiveness and "health" can be maintained.

So that the reasons for such a move are based on facts, we suggest that facilitators keeps an up-to-date record of the attendance and of the commitments that each Mastermindian makes during meetings. Thus, if one of the members is not attending the meetings or does not keep up with her/his commitments in a serious way, the facilitator has justification to end her/his participation.

Preparing for and Leading Sessions

As a Mastermind group organizer, you need to choose a location where participants will feel comfortable and safe to open themselves for input about how they are conducting their daily lives. You need to define the content of your sessions, plan the dates for the sessions, and finally, communicate with all members of the group. Each step is important, in and of itself, and requires special attention.

You should communicate with your participants before the first session, in particular about your desires and goals for the group, and prepare them for a wonderful experience. About a week before you first session, send an e-mail that contains all the information that is needed for the first meeting.

The facilitation of meetings is addressed in Chapter 3.

Creating and Maintaining a Positive, Constructive Mindset

The success of a Mastermind group primarily depends on the group's mindset. This mindset has a strong impact on both individual and collective results. The group's mindset will determine the strength and quality of the "generative field" they create together.

To help Masterminders make their way into a space where there are almost unlimited resources, it will be important for group's facilitator to "teach" them how to be **caring without being complacent.**

An effective Mastermind group's mindset also integrates a good dose of both individual and collective ambition. Each participant shows up so she/he can be successful with her/his own projects and can raise herself/himself up and exceed her/his criteria for success by working on her/his projects. This requires a great deal of determination and follow through. Procrastinators do not generally benefit from a Mastermind group (although participating in a Mastermind group can help them to take action.)

Not taking action hinders learning and change in a member. Each person should be both kind and demanding when it comes to what the other Mastermindians commit to in order to help them make their "quantum leap".

That is what we call "caring without complacency". The participants don't live in the world of the Care Bears; they are coming to meetings to find solutions with their peers, so they can take off on the path to success. It is a demanding course of action that, in all likelihood, needs to be repeated numerous times, since the participants are confronted by their mental blocks, limits (which they need to get beyond), and gray areas. Some participants become destabilized during some of the sessions and will need to be capable of showing that they have a great capacity for opening up and welcoming constructive comments so they can get constructive feedback from their peers. This mirroring effect is a wonderful gift, offered by a Mastermind group that carries out its work in the spirit of co-responsibility.

The Mastermindians should also integrate the logic of putting "others before me", or of giving before one takes. Each member should show up intending to give more than what she/he is going to take for herself/himself. It is a virtuous circle of giving; the first thing given is to the other; that creates the power behind some truly wonderful, reciprocal exchanges.

This logic of putting "the other before myself" also applies to the participants' opportunities to speak, and the time that is spent on that. In "normal" groups, it is not unusual for some people to appropriate all of the time that is to be used for talking. The Mastermind group should not be thought of as a "normal" one. Everyone shows up to first listen to the others, not to hear themselves talk. The facilitator expresses authority on this important point in terms of mindset. She/He can invoke Confucius' saying that: "If Man has a mouth and two ears, it's so he can listen twice as much as he talks."

The Mastermindians' agenda is always oriented towards action. A person has to be daring in the first place if she/he is going to be successful—Isn't that so? Therefore, the participants spend a large part of their time thinking about different plans of action. They ask each other the following questions: "How can it be done?" "How can it be done better?" They advise and challenge one another. Emulating the success of others becomes more important, and taking action becomes an obsession. At worst, none of that works. But every failure is a success in terms of learning for oneself and for the group. And each bit of learning amounts to success. This taking of action is one of the components of the responsibility that each member of the group has to demonstrate. Each individual is responsible for taking action. They also support others to take action. This spirit of co-responsibility guarantees that each member of the group can help her/his peers move forward and dare to do something new or different. Each individual takes on the mindset, "What can I do to help you take action?"

Finally, Mastermind group participants must acknowledge the principle that they can progress as human beings, along with their peers, because of the group. This requires a level of humility, some transparency, and a capacity for showing one's vulnerability. A Mastermind group is a space where each individual shares, in all honesty, her/his problems, doubts, fears, and questions. And at times, if the level of trust is high among all of the participants, some small instances of shame that might be spoiling one's life. That is where the principle of confidentiality becomes totally necessary. What is said in the group is done so under the seal of confidentiality.

And you ask me, what about humor? Like C.W. Metcalf says: "Take your work seriously but yourself lightly." Every individual allows her/his "free-spirited child" to experience life through the use of humor and self-deprecation (or self-healing). That allows the group to be more creative.

Ensure Communication and Follow-up between Meetings

For a Mastermind group to be effective is it important for each member to keep in contact with the rest of the participants so that a space for sharing can me maintained and, above all, so that participants keep up with their commitments. Thus, it is essential for the facilitator to:

* Send a follow-up e-mail that describes the milestones that were achieved at the time of the last session, and about the changes that are expected to take place before the next meeting.

* Add supplemental information, different kinds of clever things, links to web pages, and interesting books.

* Ask your participants to send you an update about their progress.

* Propose guidelines for specific development tasks.

The facilitator, who is always on the lookout for the latest technologies, can facilitate communication in her/his group by introducing new collaborative tools that are on the Internet. These tools allow a connection between the members of a group to be maintained without flooding their inboxes.

It is useful, for example, to create private online spaces with tools like Facebook, Google Group, Slack, Trello, Asana, and more. That is how members can post their profiles and photos, ask questions, share their progress, participate in discussion groups, and share documents and resources. The more connected your members are, the more they will share and collaborate.

Although in-person gatherings are effective and even preferable, the facilitator can also arrange telephone or video conferences (Skype, Hangout, Go-To-Meeting, etc.). In those cases, it is better to plan the sessions so that they last more than two hours.

Ensure the Group's Flow of Energy

Since the quality of what emerges from a group, in terms of engagement, and of the members' presence, and the strength of their goals and ambition, depends on the members' level of trust and harmonious interaction, the facilitator pays particular attention of the group's level of collective energy. Napoleon Hill already said in 1937 that a Mastermind group's facilitator's main role is that of creating harmony so that the level of energy can be increased for all the participants. His main belief was that everyone improves through sharing!

The facilitator helps create the conditions for trusting relationships so that participants feel a desire, and even a need, to advise, support, and help each other out. At the time of the meetings, she/he guides participants to the deepest levels of discussion possible and looks out for possible obstacles, such as lack of understanding, awkward interactions, psychological games, tension, or any breeding ground for conflicts that might upset the free flow of energy and compromise the harmony that exists within the group.

The group's main energy comes from its participants, their individual ambitions and the intentions they have towards the other members. The facilitator spots and injects enthusiasm into these key elements of the group's mindset. She/He increases the energy already in the system if she/he feels that the group's level of energy is low. She/He should allow brilliant, powerful sources of energy to emerge, after creating the right conditions for it to take place. She/He focuses the participants' attention on what is important, positive, and generative. Those are the conditions under which it is possible for the collective intelligence and brilliance of the group to emerge.

A Mastermind group facilitator wants to maintain a high level of energy and enthusiasm, but not too much. It is important that the energy level be sustainable and that people do not "burn out." She/He also wants to apply the basic principles for effective group facilitation: seeing to it that everyone expresses her/himself, creating an environment that is favorable for debates on differing ideas, seeing to it that the participants' roles vary, welcoming the expression of emotions in a tactful way, regulating interactions between participants, making it possible for members to let go of tensions, helping everyone to find solutions that can be put into practice, maintaining high-quality connections that favor confidence, keeping a strict watch over the time, while still being open to flexibility in that regard, etc.

Strengthening Group Members' Commitment

A group whose members don't show up on a regular basis is one that will quickly die out. Each and every participant needs to be made aware that her/his Mastermind sessions are part and parcel of an essential commitment for her/him and her/his peers. The dates that are set up for them cannot be changed, and absence is only permissible if one is having a crisis such as a health issue.

The facilitator establishes the conditions for participation in the group so that there is no doubt about just how important they are. To that end, she/he should:

* Bring in something new, from one session to the next, to maintain a high level of motivation on the part of the members.

* Encourage every group member to act as a mentor for other members of the group.

* Adapt her/his program, depending on the information gathering capacities of the system that is being used and the situation.

* Promote the motto "the one who gives also receives".

* Motivate members to be present at each session.

* Require members to be 100 % committed to their own success and that of the other members.

* Verify that all the goals that have been shared with the group have indeed been achieved.

The Development of Participants' Skills

Although this is not necessarily what Mastermindians ask for, the facilitator is also in place to promote members' growth as human beings, in addition to that as business leaders. To facilitate this growth, the facilitator should serve as an example, transmit ideas and knowledge, add a great deal to what is going on, and act as a mentor that asks for nothing in return except for members' commitment.

The ability to ask for help or to offer help without expecting anything in return are essential for benefiting fully from Mastermind groups. There is also the growth and development that comes from acknowledging one's own vulnerability in front of a group of peers. These capacities are essential for the personal development of participants in Mastermind groups. Individuals who possess these skills are often more authentic and perform at higher levels than the others!

To support the development of her/his group members' skills, the Mastermind facilitator will sometimes offer workshops targeted to improve certain abilities. She/He will choose topics that are adapted to the participants' needs and support them to take risks. The facilitator helps participants to focus on the positive aspects of challenging experience so that participants can experience the power and pleasure of turning obstacles into projects, and projects into learning experiences.

The facilitator can have outside experts intervene in the group if she/her himself does not have the specific skills that are needed for the participants to make progress. It could be someone who is well-known or not; such as a trainer in a specific area, or someone who has done something extraordinary and can give her/his testimony—someone like a highly accomplished sportsperson, for example. Some examples of such contributions from the outside can include themes such as: project management, business leadership, business design, estate management, financial placements, marketing, positive thinking, meditation, crowdfunding, financing of innovative efforts, numerical transformation, businesses trend charts, the leader's posture, etc.

Inciting the Group to Think Differently About Things

The facilitator helps the group ask good questions and be open to other points of view.

Albert Einstein pointed out that *"Insanity (consists of) doing the same thing over and over again and expecting different results."* A major part of the Mastermind group facilitator's role consists of leading participants to think in different ways by asking questions, such as:

* Can you imagine other options?

* Can you test other possibilities?

* How does one change the course of History?

* How does one interrupt the course of History?

* What re-adjustments can you make?

Applying the Tetralemma

It is amazing to see how human beings often have a tendency to analyze things from a binary point of view; that is to say, they make choices between two contradictory solutions, each one being as unsatisfactory as the other. That is what is referred to as a dilemma. It is important to realize that in every situation there is an infinite number of ways to look at things. When a dilemma surfaces in a Mastermind group, it is part of the facilitator's role to help the group consider other points of view. The "tetralemma" is a powerful format for accomplishing that. Instead of thinking in a binary way, the facilitator leads the group into thinking about other possible perspectives The difference between a dilemma and a tetralemma is illustrated below.

In binary logic, or a dilemma, there are only two possibilities:

1 – A is true; B is false.

2 – B is true; A is false.

In a tetralemma, there are four different possibilities:

1 - A is true; B is false.

2 – B is true; A is false.

3 – A and B are both true.

4 – Neither A nor B are true.

Point 3 allows one to consider two points of view at the same time, and Point 4 allows one to think about new points of view, other than A and B, at the same time that it poses the question "and if neither A nor B are true, what then?" This is a powerful way to avoid conflict and create the conditions for greater collective intelligence.

Facilitation Based on Collective Intelligence

Why should facilitation be based on collective intelligence?

Collective intelligence potentially leads to the co-creativity, co-responsibility, and co-governance that is characteristic of high performing groups. Creating collective intelligence involves establishing a framework of non-judgmental confidentiality that produces a protective "membrane" around the group.

According to Pierre Levy, every human being holds within herself/himself the capacity for contributing to a larger collective intelligence. Collective intelligence requires individual intelligence and specialized knowledge to be included in a group's interactions.

Collective intelligence results from cooperation and collaboration that is favorable for the emergence of both individual intelligence and synergy. Creating the conditions for collective intelligence to emerge is a necessity for an effective Mastermind group.

How does a facilitator support the emergence of a group's collective intelligence?

Mastermind group processes are always organized around participants sitting in a circle. This structure allows everyone to see each other and symbolizes that participant's contributions all have equal weight.

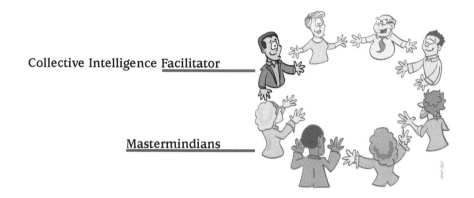

Collective Intelligence Facilitator _____

Mastermindians _____

Any time that participants are reflecting on things, or when decisions are to be made, the facilitator has them form a circle so that each one of them has a chance to express herself/himself and so that everyone is equally engaged.

During any facilitation process, participants contribute their thoughts and perspectives into the circle. It is the synergy and integration of these ideas and opinions that are the foundation of the groups' collective intelligence. It is just as important to the promotion of collective intelligence to observe periods of silence that signify reflection and gestation.

The Mastermind group facilitator is THE guardian of the circle and makes sure that its rules and framework are respected.

The facilitator also sets up time for reflection in subgroups and then re-creates the circle so there can be large-group sharing. The collective contribution of the sub-groups is a key success factor in promoting collective intelligence in the larger group.

It is worth emphasizing that, for a Mastermind group to be effective, the participants need to feel enough trust to open up to others. Thus, the Mastermind group circle is also, symbolically speaking, a "circle of trust"

What Internal State is Favorable for the Development of Collective Intelligence?

One of the questions that one might ask is "why do some groups come up with some really great things while other groups are never able to perform all that adequately?" The difference lies in the mindset of any given group. In our view, there are certain generative states that are conducive to discovering solutions and, conversely, there are degenerative states that prevent a group from coming up with anything at all.

The following process, known as the COACH state, can help a group or individual to enter a generative mindset.

Being in the COACH state is a prerequisite for facilitating and developing collective intelligence. We recommend that both individuals and groups practice the COACH state as a discipline several times a day, like a type of meditation, in order to increase their capacity for presence and generativity.

COACH is an acronym that stands for:

C Centered

O Open

A Aware

C Connected

H Hospitable

These words stand for the set of internal qualities that allow people to feel in sync with themselves and with their intentions in relation to others. For a Mastermind group facilitator, using this method is a quick way of getting herself/himself and participants into the right frame of mind necessary to produce collective intelligence. When used frequently, this tool helps to reinforce the inner state necessary for collective intelligence to emerge. It helps participants to establish a more centered, fluid, and generous state of mind.

In our view, a key part of a Mastermind group facilitator's role consists of guiding the group into the COACH state and then maintaining it through the session. A good facilitator is attentive to her/his group's mindset and intervene's whenever the group drops into a "non-generative" frame of mind, or CRASH state. The word CRASH is an acronym that stands for:

C Contraction

R Reactivity

A Analysis Paralysis

S Separation

H Hostility

The group's mindset will clearly have a strong influence on the group's dynamics and, therefore, on the actions and interactions. As the facilitator repeatedly brings the group members' attention to the quality of their mindset, they will gradually become capable of picking up on whether they are in a generative (COACH) state or non-generative (CRASH) state.

A good facilitator realizes that it is the strength of both the individual and collective COACH state that will determine the ease and productivity of the group's interaction.

Example of the COACH state

I suggest that you close your eyes and focus on your breathing. Every time you inhale, and every time you exhale, notice how your chest swells and then becomes deflated. Then place your feet firmly on the ground, relax your ankles, knees, and pelvis so your body can be as flexible as a sturdy reed. Stretch your back, shoulders, arms, forearms, and fingers. Your feet are on the ground; at the same time, your head is connected to the sky. Each part of your body makes a whole, which itself is part of another whole. Once you are centered, you should open up to the people who are in the room and open your mind to the ideas of others, so that, in the end, you will open your heart and be able to accept the perspectives of other without passing any judgment. Now that you are centered and open, be aware of the light that passes through your eyelids, pay attention to the smells that are in the room, taste what you have in your mouth, notice the pressure on your feet from the solid floor, and finally, notice how your body adjusts its position to remain balanced. Now that you are focused, open to others, and aware, you connect to yourself and with the people around you, as well with your mentors, and other people who have been important for you. They can be people like Nelson Mandela, Gandhi, Albert Einstein, Mozart, important teachers you have had, or your parents and grandparents. You can also connect with the entire field of knowledge that surrounds you. Albert Einstein said, "I didn't create my most important ideas; the ideas came *to* me." You are like a receptor that takes in a field of information that is all around us. Now that you are Centered, Open to others, Aware, and Connected to yourself and others, you will become imbued with feelings of Hospitality, which is a space where you will receive whatever is around you in an unconditional, non-judgmental way. Then, when you are ready, open your eyes, look at the rest of the group and say, "I am here. I see you."

Introducing an Intention

The act of presenting an intention consists of stating aloud what you desire to do for others or obtain for yourself. It may also include how you will achieve that and the frame of mind you will take on in order to achieve it. Stating what we want to accomplish allows us to give direction to our actions for a particular period of our lives. It allows us to clarify, solidify and our choices and decisions. It is important to keep in mind, however, that an intention is not the same thing as a goal. It acts at a level that is higher than that of a goal. Intentions function more at the emotional level and establish a particular mindset. Setting intention entails a mental adjustment when it comes to the way that one approaches what she/he is going to do.

When we have no clear intention, we can easily let ourselves be carried away by whatever is happening around us. Without intention, it is difficult to take advantage of opportunities that emerge from moment to moment. Our mind begins to roam and we miss out on opportunities that may be right in front of us.

Examples of Intention:

* Finding solutions for other members of the group.

* Being authentic and showing my vulnerability.

* Honestly expressing my opinions.

This notion of intention is applicable to every area of life. For example, when tennis players go to return one's serve, they have an intention about what spot they want to return the ball before their opponent even serves it. That allows them to mobilize their bodies, out of anticipation, and to coordinate their movements so they can send the ball where they want to. Actors in a theater, before they go back out on the stage, have already defined how they are going to play their part. During a concert, if the musician or singer has to play or sing a happy tune, she/he puts herself/himself in a joyous frame of mind, and then her/his fingers do the rest.

Similarly, a Mastermind group facilitator defines her/his overall intention for the group as well as for each group session. The facilitator also asks each Mastermindian to specify what she/he wants and expects from her/his participation in the group, and what she/he expects from each session. The facilitator then helps participants to determine the mindset with which she/he will achieve those intentions and expectations. The facilitator stimulates participants to exchange ideas about their intentions, and to write them down in a notebook or journal. She/He also encourages participants to continually raise their expectations, explore aspects of their mindset that have brought success in other instances, and to support one another in their intentions.

Some intentions that reinforce the mindset necessary for a Mastermind group to develop its capacity for collective intelligence include:

* Connecting to oneself and to others.

* Being open to the ideas of others, at the same time that you allow prejudices to fall by the wayside.

* Being focused on the present and staying in the here and now.

* Being open-minded, at the same time that you don't pass judgment on others.

* Being able to distance yourself from your ideas.

* Being open to taking action, commitment, and co-responsibility.

* Being more trustworthy and more creative.

* Having a capacity for using silence as a resource to bring about the emergence of intelligent ideas.

* Being accepting and hospitable towards ourselves and towards others.

One of the fundamental tasks of collective intelligence is to create a state of readiness in people, in which they let go (of their egos), and, at the same time, pay a great deal of attention to what they intend to accomplish.

The facilitator's capacity for inducing an appropriate attitude in the groups' participants allows hem to gather perspectives and pick up on the personal attributes that are characteristic of themselves, at the same time that they remain connected to the needs of the group. Each person is there for herself/himself, and present for the others, so that she/he can support the others without passing judgment or showing any prejudices towards them. That is when a Mastermind group manifests that famous collective brain that Napoleon Hill talked about, which allows it to generate something that is greater than what a single person would be able to imagine on her/his own. It creates a situation where $1 + 1 > 2$. That is to say, that the whole is greater than the sum of its parts.

2.2 The Facilitator's Preparation

The facilitator is responsible for the structuring and managing the Mastermind group's process so that each participant can succeed with their goals. The facilitator defines her/his Mastermind group's general intention and guides the collective dynamics. She/He also has to be ready to offer what is going to be pertinent and effective for the group. In this sense, the facilitator needs to prepare herself/himself as much as her/his intervention.

The facilitator carefully organizes everything, based on five key points:

1) The facilitator should be clear about her/his motivations for wanting to be at the center of this supportive process. Without entering into a discussion about it at this point, everyone who lends her/his support other people in this way should have an interest in working on herself/himself, too. This will help her/him to clarify her/his reasons for helping other people. It's possible that she/he will receive remuneration, but money should not be the primary goal of leading a Mastermind group. By clarifying her/his own intentions, and by studying any of her/his gray areas, the facilitator will achieve a high level of alignment and congruence. This also helps the her/him to support the group members in clarifying their own motivations and goals for being in the group.

2) The facilitator prepares herself/himself by raising her/his level of "concentration". She/He focuses on the services that she/he is going to offer to the participants. This concentration, allied with a deep kind of focusing, allows her/him to better place herself/himself in a "meta" position, which consists of observing what is happening from a wise witnessing position. From this point of unattached observation, she/he looks for the things that are going on that have meaning for the Mastermindians. This high-level of concentration and focusing allow her/him to detect salient, significant, important information that will lead to the participants' personal and professional growth.

3) The facilitator ensures that she/he will carry out the effective management of workshops and processes that she/he is going to offer to the Mastermindians. She/He can use the interactive formats suggested in this book or offer different procedures. Whatever processes the facilitator chooses she/he should make her/his fullest and best efforts. Therefore, she/he should carefully plan and study ahead of time the processes with which he/she will lead the group. Remember that the job of facilitation is mainly carried out by coaches and consultants who have been trained in the areas of group dynamics and the facilitation of collective intelligence.

4) The facilitator strives to bring about strong emotional changes in the Mastermindians. Intellectual understanding is not, most of the time, enough to trigger off an effective course of action. Learning is not only a cognitive process, but also a complex process of somatic integration. Emotions lead to learning and decision-making. We advise the facilitator to choose group processes that engage the hearts, feelings and emotions of group members in order to have the fullest impact.

5) Finally, the facilitator works on her/his overall goal for the group. What will she/he offer that will bring about the greatest benefit and have the greatest positive impact for each member, over the long run? She/He defines her/his vision for the group and aligns herself/himself fully with that vision. The notion of alignment is important when it comes to increasing motivation and determination. Thus, at the time that the facilitator undertakes the process of defining her/his vision, and her/his alignment in relation to it, she/he clarifies her/his mission and role. That is, the person that she/he should be, in order to carry out her/his vision.

VISION	AMBITION
What I want, as facilitator, for other people, for the group, and more generally, for society.	What I want to get for me when I put myself at the service of the participants ? What is my goal, and what ambitions do I have for the participants in "my" Mastermind group?
MISSION	**ROLE**
What I must do as facilitator so that my vision becomes reality, since I am the only one able to make a high-level contribution to the group. What I must do so that the participants carry out their high-level goals, and so that they will be aligned with their own ambitious vision.	The position I must take and the person I must be so that I bring about the realization of my vision for my Mastermind group. What the Mastermindians should hear, see, and feel when they look at and listen to me.

When the group has enough experiences in common, the facilitator can fill in this same chart so the group can clarify its goals vis-à-vis themselves and the other participants. This approach of aligning with the vision can be repeated at regular intervals to make sure that participants are always in line with their goals, both individually and collectively.

2.3 Facilitator Profile

The facilitator's primary tool is, of course, herself/himself, her/his own ambitions, and her/his goals for participants. She/He should be organized, flexible, a good listener, empathetic, caring, and dynamic.

Here are some elements of the profile possessed by a good facilitator:

Positive, demanding,
congruence, curious,
open minded

Smiling, humor, welcoming

Leadership

Push to action
Commitment

Love people

Agile, aware, flexible

2.4 The Facilitator's Posture

Facilitating the development of collective intelligence in a Mastermind group requires the facilitator to assume a posture different from that of a teacher (or that of an expert) to her/his student. In other words, she/he is not the one who knows bringing her/his expertise to those who do not know. Even if she/he has seen ahead of time that she/he can develop participants' skills, she/he is not there to give a lecture but to put the participants in the role of actors in a process. The facilitator leads reflective kinds of processes and proposes procedures and methodologies (as well as new ways to look at things) that will cause the group's collective intelligence to emerge. She/He assumes, inside of this framework, a rather subdued posture based on curiosity, listening to the others, and allowing herself/himself to have the right to make mistakes and exercise humility.

However, as an animator of the group, he must at certain moments put himself in the position to enforce the group's framework, rules, values (respect, trust, commitment, conviviality, etc.). The facilitator needs to remind the Mastermindiens of their commitments, with respect to the meetings and the actions they plan to implement between sessions. She/He is also there to make the group grow in skills. Moreover, a lot of participants actually choose the facilitator for who she/he is before they decide on what Mastermind to join. They do indeed gravitate towards a charismatic personality who has leadership skills. That places that facilitator in an elevated position, in relation to them.

Throughout a Mastermind session, the facilitator should move back and forth between a subdued and and more proactive posture. This requires a great deal of flexibility, good self-awareness, and the experience to know when she/he should actually do both of those things.

Chapter 3

How Should a Mastermind Meeting Be Facilitated?

3.1 Why Is the Hot Seat Such a Powerful Tool?

What Does It Mean to Go on the Hot Seat?

When a Mastermindian goes into the "middle of the circle" so she/he can state her/his question and ask for opinions and advice from the other group members, she/he has gone onto the hot seat (renamed the "love seat" by Robert Dilts).

Here is the authentic account that was written by one of the authors of this book after he was on the hot seat.

I was standing next to the paperboard. There were about 10 or so entrepreneurs and business leaders in front of me who were getting ready to listen to me. We'd just experienced what coaching is all about (see an explanation of this later in this chapter, and back on page ...). All the attention was focused on me. I turned the recorder on my phone. I barely had 10 minutes to present my situation and strategy for dealing with it. The timer function on a Smartphone was activated. The Smartphone was going to go off in 10 minutes. I was "on stage" during that time, as I explained my vision, and the question that I had, at that time...

I was prepared, of course. I knew which ideas I was going to present. I came up with a few outlines that would illustrate what I was feeling. I was very familiar with the dilemma that was gnawing away at me, and for which I needed clarifications. I then took off with it. I developed my theme, jotted some words on the board, drew things, and responded to some questions to clarify things for the others, above all, after I used the jargon that is characteristic of my profession. The facilitator made sure that no debate arose—it wasn't the right moment for that.

At the end of 10 minutes a sound went off that signaled that the time that had been allotted to me was over. I didn't stop right at that instant—To bring everything to a close, I threw out the key question, then jotted things down on the paperboard, and ended my arguments. I sat back down and picked up a pen and some papers.

This was the second step in the process: Each one of my Mastermindian colleagues took a turn to talk. They were only supposed to express their impressions about what I had shared. What kind of sensations, vibrations, and images did my presentation cause to emerge? In this case, it was an emotional brain that was at work. It did not (at that point) have anything to do with logical reasoning and analysis. No discussion was carried out—there was just a random going around the circle, while everyone observed the need to stay on the "feelings".

Even as the recording was going on, I scratched out all of the feedback I had received on one of the pieces of paper that I had. I also scratched out, as quickly as I could, any interpretation of what I had heard, just the ideas I caught as they flew by me. It only took a little longer than 5 minutes to go around the whole group

I started to talk again. What was my reaction to all of their impressions? Was I surprised? Did I find it encouraging? How did everyone's comments affect me? There was no discussion about it.

The third stage, also timed (10 minutes), began. The recording got underway; I had paper and a pen in my hand. Not in any particular order, and not seeming to follow any rules, my colleagues bombarded me with questions, from the most pertinent to the most preposterous, from the most concrete to the most unexpected, from the most strategic to those that are only secondary. All questions were welcome. All the bouncing back and forth of ideas promoted the emergence of creativity. The questions burst forth, from every direction, in a creative kind of disorder. I took note of things and scribbled them out; I listened to questions but did not respond to them. I stored them in my mind. The time would come when I would make a dry analysis of them. My peers brought up a lot of things I was concerned about when they questioned me; but they also brought out some things I had pushed out of my awareness, or whose existence I didn't even know about… Their questions also, of course, led me to think about issues or themes with which I am perfectly familiar. This phase of the process then ended; I felt dizzy.

I talked again, for less than five minutes. What did all of what took place stir up in me? What were my feelings? Did my thinking become more advanced? Were new avenues opened up to me?

After all of the questioning, comments came out from around the group: Each of my colleagues started to talk again. Once again, I listened, took notes, and made a recording. At that time, the facilitator asked everyone to say to me, "If I were in your place, here is what I would do, here is the first three actions I would commit to." My peers switched from a posture of questioning, so that things could be heard and clarified, to that of concrete propositions. The ideas, advice, and challenges burst forth from all directions... Some people were inspired by ideas of others so they could then make new proposals. In less than 10 minutes, I wrote down a list of actions that I was going to weigh, make choices about, appropriate for myself, amend, and eliminate... later on! It's a sure thing that I am going to carry out some of them.

I started to talk again so I could give my feedback about what went on during this stage. I emphasized what I found surprising, what troubled me, what I found encouraging, what I intended to carry out, starting with this meeting until the next one that took place. And, of course, I was greatly thankful for the opportunity.

We quickly went around the circle one last time before we ended. Everyone shared how she/he experienced my time on the hot seat, and what all of us got out of it for her/his own advancement...

In less than an hour, I accumulated a huge amount of raw material I could use for my business, 17 pages of notes, recordings that can be listened to again, and a plan of action that could be implemented... I knew that, at the time of our next meeting, my allies were going to want me to tell them what had happened after they had given me their advice. That kind of support helped me get my head together so I could move forward.

I became dizzy from all of the feedback and haven't been able to recover from the profound impact that the experience has had on me. It tired me out!

The Hot Seat is the Main Focus of a Mastermind Group

One would have to assert that there would be no Mastermind group without a hot seat. That is what one goes there for!

The hot seat procedure, as described above, lasts about an hour. It is THE key process that takes place in a Mastermind group. We will take it up and analyze it in greater detail later on. There are other processes carried out in the same spirit during the facilitation of a Mastermind group, which last from 30 minutes to 2 hours:

* The classic hot seat	Lasts about an hour
* "Johnny bombing"	Lasts about 30 min
* The Coaching Circle, based on Theory U[1]	Lasts about 1 hour 30 minutes
* The Pro Action Café	Lasts about 2 h
* Co-development workshop	Lasts about 1 h 30 min
* The World Café	Lasts about 2 h

Besides the "hot seat" activity, the facilitator brings in other tools that reflect her/his experience and orientation, which she/he will use for the facilitation of her/his Mastermind group. Like, for example, what is listed on the following non-exhaustive list:

* Going around the circle so each participant can quickly mention her/his good news…

* Doing a role play around a participant's specific issue, in which she/he plays her/his own role (a facilitator who in familiar with this method can draw her/his inspiration from social theater)…

* Making methodological contributions that are consistent with the needs and expectations of the participants (forms of training that can be adjusted quickly)…

* Asking a Mastermindian to introduce what amounts to good professional practice, even for one's overall life, or the kind of wisdom which is likely to be of interest to all of her/his colleagues…

---

1   Scharmer Otto, La théorie de U, renouveler le leadership, 2016, Collegence and Yves Michel Editions.

* Having a specialist carry out a calibrated intervention, or a witness who has high added value in relation to participants' expectations. The expert becomes the meeting's "exceptional host"…

* Organizing a discussion on the subject of business management, marketing, networking, business finances, etc…

* Requiring that all Mastermindians go through an uplifting experience, such as traveling, participating in some sport, escaping into nature…

* Etc.

The only condition that the facilitator has to abide by is that of focusing on powerful procedures and interventions that offer a great deal of added value. The goal remains that of allowing each participant to step up to and go through the highest stage of development.

What is the Most Effective Hot Seat Method?

Going onto the hot seat is what the Mastermind group process is mainly focused on; it is its atomic core. Mastermind group facilitators use different types of procedures so that business leaders and entrepreneurs can make progress in their groups, but going onto the hot seat is probably the most effective activity. As far as we are concerned, it's the essential difference between a Mastermind group and other types of groups.

Let's break down the concept of the hot seat which was presented in the earlier account made by one of the authors. The method we advocate, and which is illustrated on the following pages, places great emphasis on the principles of collective intelligence. Count on "Johnny" being on the hot seat for about an hour.

Note: *In this chapter, "Johnny" is used as the nickname for any person on the hot seat.*

Steps	Duration	Procedures
Step 1	10 minutes	Johnny stands up in front of his peers. He can use a flipchart if he wants. He explains his situation, project, dilemma, and issue. He writes, draws, talks, gestures, etc.

Some participants ask clear, concise questions to get clarification of everything. Johnny gives clear, concise answers. No discussion follows. The facilitator makes sure that that rule is respected.

Johnny asks the group a question. |
| | | The timer goes off after 10 minutes. Johnny ends his presentation as soon as it does. The breathless pace has delivered results; Johnny has gotten straight to the point. |
| **Step 2** | 10 minutes | After about 30 seconds of silence, when everyone "connects" with herself/himself, everyone else, in turn, lets Johnny know what she/he is feeling (and nothing other than that). The rest listen. It is indeed a matter of sharing feelings, an exercise which at times is difficult; a lot of the participants often switch over, too quickly, to the analysis of the problem. The feelings issue is one that has to do with perceptions and energy, and the effect they have on the body, etc.

Johnny takes notes without responding and records what he wants from all of the feedback so he can make use of it at a later time. |
| | 3 minutes | Johnny shares some feedback, based on his impressions of what has just been said to him. |

Steps	Duration	Procedures
Step 3	10 minutes	In no particular order, and without any negotiating, each Mastermindian throws out questions as soon as they come to mind. Every person bounces off of the questions of the others and proposes new explorations into the issue at hand. Both open- and close-ended questions are welcome, as well as those that might seem kind of far-fetched, in addition to those that are obviously pertinent to and specifically address the issue. No discussion follows—just questions that burst out of everybody's mouth. Johnny takes notes without responding and records what he wants from all of the feedback so he can make use of it at a later time.
		The timer goes off at the end of 10 minutes.
	3 minutes	Johnny gives some feedback, based on his impressions of what has just been said to him. What surprised him? What had an impact on him? What gray areas or new perspectives surface?

Steps	Duration	Procedures
Step 4	10 minutes	Each participant takes a turn and speaks: "If I were in your shoes, here are the three things I would do, first and foremost." No discussions take place at this point. But if one of the Mastermindians triggers off a key idea in the mind of her/his peer, she/he starts to talk again: "Oops! A fourth proposal has just come into my mind, which seems as if it's very important to include." Johnny takes notes without responding and records what he wants from all of the feedback so he can make use of it at a later time.
		The timer goes off at the end of 10 minutes.
	3 minutes	Johnny gives feedback based on his impressions about what has just been said to him. He shares those commitments or initiatives that he intends to follow up on when he is on the hot seat, so he can improve his situation and speed up his progress and the success of his project. He expresses his gratitude to the group.
Step 5	3 minutes	End of the process. The facilitator quickly goes around the table one more time to give everyone an opportunity to share what this exercise has been like for her/him.

The hot seat, which is the key component in the work that is carried out in a Mastermind group, is part of a process that is particularly beneficial. For the individual who is "grilled" (Johnny), it is an exercise in synthesis (presentation inside of a few minutes), humility (I listen to opinions, some of which run counter to my view of things, and learning I have discovered new courses of action that I hadn't envisaged). For her/his co-Mastermindians who listen, make observations, and contribute, it is a matter of gymnastics that involve attention, coaching, advice, and creativity. The Mastermind group allows Johnny, as well as his peers, to develop human skills that are very important for her/his daily professional activities; in particular, those of listening and making contributions that have added value!

Does the Amount of Time Seem Like It's Not Enough?
Then You Have to Do Some Johnny Bombing!

"Johnny Bombing" is a quicker, more intense, more powerful, and perhaps a more destabilizing version of the "hot seat". It is used in a group that already knows how to carry out the latter. This procedure lasts about 30 minutes. Johnny has to confirm that it's OK with him if his peers would happen to upset him, since the amount of time allotted for such sessions leaves little room for fainthearted interventions.

Prior to "Johnny Bombing", the facilitator takes the precaution of easing the group into the COACH[2] state and reminds the participants, before they undertakes the work, of several of the ingredients necessary for the group to succeed:

* It needs to get straight to the point and avoid all useless verbiage.

* It needs to make sure that the time each participant spends talking is the same amount allotted to every other participant.

* It should engage only in exchanges and questions that will be of use to Johnny.

* It should dare to make a forceful assertion regarding what is important.

* The participants should admit if they don't know something, or that an idea or ideas may not emerge.

* Every participant should be authentic as she/he shares "her/his" own truth.

It is useful to remind participants, before getting started, of the basic principle of "caring without complacency".

When a Mastermindian makes an intervention during this process, her/his comments should be appropriate; any "criticisms" directed at Johnny, must be made of respectfully and should be directed toward the way he works and is taking action. It is not Johnny himself who is being called into question—it's his activity that is the center of attention. That's the meaning of the expression "caring without complacency". It amounts to using precautionary language. For example, a Mastermindian might say: "Johnny, I'm going to offer an opinion that you might perceive of as severe, but I think that the initiative you are talking about, might lead to disaster, bla, bla, bla..." This introduction sets up an opening for Johnny: it's his initiative that's being called into question, not Johnny himself. The one who is intervening then develops her/his comments by disassociating the object of her/his criticism from the person of Johnny. Here's another way of presenting it:

2   See Page 70

"I think that this project that you have presented to us doesn't have much of a chance of succeeding because..." Johnny will filter through all of the opinions and will make his decisions in light of the different suggestions that have been offered. He still needs to listen to every opinion without thinking that it's a personal attack. It is all about "caring without complacency".

Methodologically speaking, "Johnny Bombing" is a hyper-dynamic hot seat. The facilitator asks Johnny if he wants to be handled with kid gloves or stirred up by the other Mastermindians in the group. Johnny may answer: "Come on, leave me be. I feel like I should have my safety belt on today. Just act cool—I don't want to get all that upset today."

Johnny "gets up on stage", takes out his cell phone, activates its dictaphone function, and records the exchanges. He quickly explains his situation, tells everybody what he needs, and what his question is.

The Mastermindians then ask questions to get clarification and nothing more. Johnny can write notes on a sheet of paper or on a paperboard, but he doesn't have to. He faces his colleagues and looks at and listens to them (their attitudes and expressions are also meaningful and offer information).

The Mastermindians review issues, proposals, and impressions inside of a raucous kind of disorder, which is characteristic of creativity and the emergence of ideas. All the talking comes out of right, left, and center, in a way that seems chaotic. It eventually comes to an end with the raising of a hand. Prior to that, it might seem like simply a jumble of words; but it is, in reality, one that is generative and creative.

At the end of the session, Johnny shares his feelings and gives feedback to his colleagues; he thanks them for their contributions, ideas, and the gifts that they have given him. He concludes by making a commitment to the group that he will take action.

The reason that this "strong arm" version is important is that it takes less time that the basic version. It allows less crucial issues to be addressed in quicker fashion. Johnny Bombing lasts about 30 minutes; and a maximum of 10 members take part in it. It allows for interactions that are very stimulating and can generate a great many ideas. There is always the risk that the activity might turn into a bunch of racket.

Johnny Bombing is suitable where the people involved are veterans at working in collective intelligence groups. As soon as such a Mastermind group meets, it assumes the attitude of "caring without complacency". Johnny Bombing can become the usual form that the hot seat takes. Nevertheless, the facilitator must pay attention to the fact that there is a risk that the intellectual dimension associated with the activity might gain the upper hand during this quick exercise,. It is important that space for emotions is also given when it comes to exchanges in a Mastermind group.

As with the other hot seat procedures, making a recording of what goes on allows one to preserve a trace of what is being shared so it can be used at a later time. It is all the more necessary during Johnny Bombing since Johnny doesn't have enough time to take notes of all the ideas and advice that are thrown at him in rapid succession. Not taking notes gives Johnny the chance to remain fully present with his partners because then he is in visual contact with them, which is something that will have a very special kind of emotional impact on him.

3.2 How a Coaching Circle Should Be Used

The coaching circle is a co-coaching format that is used in groups. It was developed by Otto Scharmer and is based on Theory U. It is a comprehensive method that allows one to work on personal and business issues, and any other kind of project. This method requires that the facilitator have in-depth experience with and a mastery of the process.

The "descent into U", proposed by Otto Scharmer, is a "private" phenomenon, in the sense that it is carried out inside of one's mind. The discordant voices of cynicism, judgment, and fear are set aside. This state of inner vigilance allows a mindset, heart, and desire, which are more open, to emerge. The base of the U corresponds to a very high-quality state of presence in which one's relationship to the world, and letting oneself go, allows her/him to be exceptionally receptive to the future that is starting to emerge... This notion of an emerging future is one of Theory U's key concepts: the future is in the process of materializing; what comes right after can make a difference.

The coaching circle is usually made up of four or five people; but just like in the case of the hot seat, it is possible to enlarge it so that it has eight or nine, some of whom would be "disciplined" participants. Each one of them only talks when it is her/her turn.

Johnny comes out on stage and presents his situation, project, and challenge. The project has to be a current, concrete one, and it has to be an important one. It has to be a project that Johnny really wants to carry out, and which falls within the scope of his skills and responsibilities. Johnny then makes a clear request for help from the group.

During the entire descent to the bottom of the U, the participants (called co-coaches when Theory U is being employed) never attempt to solve Johnny's problem. They content themselves with just opening up all of their senses so they can completely pick up on what Johnny is saying and on the "field" where his situation is located. They allow themselves to be invaded by their impressions. What are they feeling? What are they experiencing? What kind of story are they listening to? What do they see?

What images appear in their minds? What comparisons or metaphors does Johnny's story inspire or create in them? What gestures, designs, movements, and even dances, do they want to carry out at this point? What emerges, in the large sense of the word, and what allows Johnny to better understand his situation, and what should do about it?

Here is the process, broken down into stages:

Steps	Duration	Procedures
Step 1	15 minutes	Johnny presents his situation. The Mastermindians listen. All of them concentrate on his impressions, on the "field" created by Johnny, as well as on his needs and his issue.
	3 minutes	There is a moment of silence. Each person listens more closely and becomes "more in the moment" so they can help Johnny as much as they can. Each one of them takes the time to focus, notice what is resonating, the synergies, and what is emerging. All of that is meaningful.
Step 2	15 minutes	Questions for clarification of the issue (attention, no opinions or advice should be offered!): * About the situation: What challenges, or what major issues do you have to go up against? * About the others: How do the other individuals who are actively involved see the situation? * About intention: What kind of future are you trying to create? * About skills/knowledge… What do you need to learn? * About hang-ups: What do you need to leave behind, let go of, abandon?

Steps	Duration	Procedures
Step 2	15 minutes	* About needs: What type of help do you need? * About your impressions: How do you see the situation? Is there a metaphor for it, or a gesture associated with it? This list is, of course, non-exhaustive.
	3 minutes	No one moves; tranquility reigns. Each person becomes connected to the situation, to its "field", to her/his impressions, while listening to her/his heart. Each of them looks for things that resonate with the situation. What images, metaphors, impressions, and gestures surface? Everyone tries to remain open-hearted and open-minded, and willing to help.
Step 3	10 minutes	Mirroring effect. Each Mastermindian offers what emerges in her/him to Johnny: image, story, anecdote, metaphor (comparison), symbols, impressions, movement, gesture, dance, song, noise, silence, designs, information, other things. But never advice!
Step 4	3 minutes	Johnny's feedback. Johnny clarifies his situation, now that he has received all of the gifts that he can from his partners in responsibility.
	20 minutes	Generative dialogue. The Mastermindians discuss Johnny's issue amongst themselves (Johnny only intervenes if they make comments that he finds totally unacceptable). As if they are experts when it comes to his situation, they look for ideas and solutions so that Johnny can come out victorious. The dialogue can be described as "generative", that is to say, open and caring; no attempts are made to convince the others (or Johnny).

Steps	Duration	Procedures
Step 4	20 minutes	Each participant relies on the ideas and propositions of the others so that her/his line of thought and suggestions can be improved on. All of them are careful not to assume an attitude of "I know better than the others" and to remain in a situation of parity and co-responsibility, which is only meant to serve Johnny's interests. Johnny assumes the posture where he lets things emerge (the opening up of his heart, body, and mind). A single, good idea, which emerges, is worth more than a thousand irrelevant ideas. Reminder: Each participant remains in contact with her/his high level of presence and in contact with a new, emerging future. Variations on this stage: * Johnny can intervene freely. * The Mastermindians talk to Johnny and not amongst themselves.
Step 5	10 minutes	Feedback: How does Johnny see his situation now, and what was his impression of the meeting? He explains how what has just transpired has contributed to his situation (how he might implement some of the suggestions). The experience of each Mastermindian. Thank yous and sincere acknowledgment for the help.
	2 minutes	Going along with the tenets of Theory U, each person is invited to write down, in a personal notebook, what she/he has learned and the decisions she/he has made and about the progress that has been made. That allows one to raise her/his awareness about what she/he has learned, and to make better decisions, with a view to the future.

The Theory U coaching circle is a process that is a bit drawn out; that is to say, it is a bit slower than the hot seat. It takes about an hour and a half to carry out the process. It is one during which one lets time run its course, ideas are allowed to calmly emerge, and moments of silence are observed so that a better connection can be made with others, with Johnny, and the generative field. It is a process which, furthermore appeals to the Mastermindians' sensibilities, their skills in connecting with others, but also with an emerging future. It is a format that is well-suited for participants who don't want to be shaken up too much, or who need some time to involve themselves in the process, or who favor slowness over quickness.

3.3 How the "Pro Action Café"[3] Should Be Used

The "Pro Action Café" is a collective intelligence tool that turns all group participants into experts, who are needed to make sure that a project moves forward. It allows every one of them to strengthen connections and enhances all of their current knowledge and skills. It is a cross between the World Café and the Open Forum.

The Pro Action Café facilitation format allows one-fourth, even as many as one-third of the people present to address the entire group with a question, issue, or problem that has come up in the carrying out of a project, and to benefit from the contributions and feedback of the other participants.

This is a very instructive format, as much for "Johnny", who discovers other ways to look at his situation and to find solutions, as for those with whom he is consulting. Johnny's situation will resonate with them, to a very great degree.

What takes place in a Pro action Café is similar to what transpires in a World Café. In the latter, reflection is carried out on oneself, in the service of "us", while in the former, reflection is carried out by "us", in the service of "me".

The Pro Action Café can be a good alternative to the hot seat when the number of participants is large (> 9). It takes almost 2 hours to go through all of its phases, which are listed below:

---

3   Attributed to Rainer von Leoprechting and Rita Baeck.

Creation of the group

Timing: 5 minutes

What: The COACH state.

Who: The facilitator guides the group to the COACH state.

Tools and support: 3 P's rule.

Sharing

Timing: 10 minutes

What: The facilitator helps identify the participants who want to present their project and the problem that they have encountered with it. She/He also supports the selected participants with the formulation of the question that they will ask about their project.

Who: The facilitator and the people who have brought their project to the group for consideration.

Tools and support: Flip Chart.

Choice of projects

Timing: 5 minutes

What: The projects to be presented are selected. Given the available time, only 1/4 to 1/3 of the participants can be given support for their projects. The rest of the group will be "consultants".

Who: The participants.

The facilitator helps the group to make the selection of projects.

If necessary, the group can simply apply the "first come, first serve" rule.

Tools and support: Flip Chart.

Presentation about how a Pro Action Café works

Timing: 5 minutes

What: The facilitator explains that those who have brought in their projects will go to a table, which has consultants sitting around it. There should be a balanced distribution between the number of consultants surrounding the table, and those who have brought in projects.

Four questions will be asked. The consultants will change tables between each of the questions to ensure the mixing and the synergy of ideas.

20 minutes will be devoted to each question in order to maintain a rhythm during sessions.

When new consultants come to the table, the one who is bringing her/his project to it comes up with a synthesis, based on what has already been done.

Who: The facilitator.

Tools and support: Flip Chart.

Question 1

Timing: 15 minutes

What: Question 1: What is the issue behind the issue (or the search), which is behind the question?

Who: The facilitator gives the question to the group.

The consultants pose the question to the person who has brought her/his project that is to be addressed by their circle.

The person who has brought in the project writes down everything that she/he understands on the Flip Chart, at the same time, structuring the responses.

Tools and support: Flip Chart; Colored felt-tip pens.

Changing of tables

Timing: 2 minutes

What: The consultants change tables. Those who have brought in their projects stay at the same table.

Reproduction of comments

Timing: 1 minute

What: The person who has brought in the project takes 1 minute to reproduce, for her/his new consultants, what has already emerged.

Who: The person who brings in the project.

Tools and support: Flip Chart used for Question 1.

Question 2

Timing: 15 minute

What: Question 2: What is missing from my project, from my question, from my thinking?

Who: The facilitator gives the question to the group.

The consultants ask their questions to the person who has brought her/his project to their table.

The person who has brought in the project writes everything that she/he understands on the Flip Chart, thereby giving a structure to the responses answers.

Tools and support: Paperboard.

Changing of tables

Timing: 2 minutes

What: The consultants change tables. Those who have brought in their projects stay at the same table.

Reproduction of comments

Timing: 1 minute

What: The person who has brought in the project takes 1 minute to reproduce, for her/his new consultants, what has already emerged.

Who: The person who brings in the project.

Tools and support: Flip Chart used for Questions 1 and 2.

Question 3

Timing: 15 minute

What: Question 3: What am I learning about myself, about my project? What are the next steps? What kind of help do I need?

Who: The facilitator poses the question to the group.

The consultants pose the question to the person who has brought in the project for their table. The person who has brought in the project write everything that she/he understands on the Flip Chart, thereby giving a structure to the responses.

Tools and support: Flip Chart.

Changing of tables

Timing: 2 minutes

What: The consultants change tables. Those who have brought in their projects stay at the same table.

Reproduction of comments

Timing: 1 minute

What: The person who has brought in the project takes 1 minute to reproduce, for her/his new consultants, what has already emerged.

Who: The person who brings in the project.

Tools and support: FlipChart used for Questions 1, 2 and 3.

Question 4

Timing: 15 minute

What: Question 4:

What am I grateful for? What are my next steps?

Who: The person who has brought in the project reflects about what she/he appreciates, that has come from the consultants, and about the next steps she/he is going to commit to, in front of the group.

Tools and support: Flip Chart.

Sharing

Timing: 20 minute

What: While in a circle, everyone shares what she/he is grateful for, what she/he has learned.

Everyone answers the following questions:

 *What have each of us learned for ourselves, about our projects, and for the entire group?

 *What do we want to retain from the exchanges and tools that can be used when it comes to our own efforts?

 *What am I grateful for? What are my next steps?

Who: The participants.

The facilitator

Ending of the Session

Timing: 5 minute

What: Closing down of the Pro Action Café.

Who: The facilitator

3.4 How the World Café[4] Should Be Used

The World Café is a collective intelligence process that allows constructive dialogue and the sharing of knowledge and ideas between participants, so that they can come up with a common vision, by working on common goal and defining concrete actions. This process re-creates the ambiance of a café because its participants are spread out into sub-groups. Except for the host of any given table, the participants change tables at regular intervals. The host's role is that of reproducing what is said between each question, at her/his table, and at the time of the group's final feedback. In a World Café, reflection is carried out from the point of view of "me", in the service of "us", while in a Pro Action Café, reflection is carried out by "us", in the service of "me".

The World Café derives all of its meaning from a Mastermind group, especially since it leads the group to reflect on themes or subjects that it wants to address during the same. The tricky thing about the World Café is that the participants have to come up with good questions.

The World Café can take place as long as there is the right amount of people (> 9). All phases of the process listed below take about 2 hours to accomplish:

Creation of the group
Timing: 5 minute

What: COACH state.

Who: The facilitator guides the group to the COACH state.

Tools and support: The 3P's rule.

Presentation about how a World Café group works
Timing: 5 minute

What: The facilitator explains that World Café is a collective intelligence tool that allows a group to reflect on a common issue project or vision.

There will be 5 people at each table. Each sub-group will respond to 3 questions. The participants of the sub-groups are required to change tables, except for one person. That person has a special role—that of the host for a particular table, so she/he does not change tables.

The host's job is to review with the new arrivals to the table what has been said at that table in response to the previous question(s). The host will also make a summary to the group at the end of each of the 3 questions. Each question is addressed over a period of 20 minutes.

Who: The facilitator.

Tools and support: Flip Chart.

---

4   http://www.theworldcafe.com.

Question 1

Timing: 20 minute

What: A question is defined by the facilitator. For example:

* When do you feel alone when you are carrying out your work as a senior executive?
* What limits your development?
*What is the driving force behind your internal engine?

Who: The facilitator asks the question. The participants in each sub-group respond simultaneously to Question 1.

The host at each table writes the responses on a Flip Chart.

Tools and support: Flip Chart
Colored Felt-tip pens.

Changing of tables

Timing: 2 minutes

What: Except for the host at each table, all participants change to another table, taking care to mix with new people.

Review of previous comments

Timing: 2 minutes

What: Once participants are seated as part of a new sub-group, the host at the table takes 2 minutes to review what has been said at her/his table by previous participants.

Who: The host

Tools and support: Flip Chart used in conjunction with the presentation of Question 1.

Question 2

Timing: 20 minute

What: Another question is defined by the facilitator. For example:

* What are the skills that you need?
* What do you need to be successful?
* What obstacles do you usually encounter as you go along?
* What is the driving force behind your internal engine?

Who: The facilitator asks the question.

The participants in each sub-group respond simultaneously to Question 2.

The host at the table writes the responses on a Flip Chart.

Tools and support: Flip Chart. Colored Felt-tip pens.

Changing of tables

Timing: 2 minutes

What: Except for the host at each table, all participants change to another table, taking care to mix with new people.

Review of previous comments

Timing: 2 minutes

What: Once participants are seated as part of a new sub-group, the host at the table takes 2 minutes to review what has been said at her/his table by previous participants.

Who: The host

Tools and support: Flip Chart used in conjunction with the presentation of Questions 1 and 2.

Question 3

Timing: 20 minute

What: A final question is defined by the facilitator. For example:
* If you get beyond the present challenge, what will that allow you to expect?
* How do you visualize what "success" looks like?
* What is your goal?

Who: The facilitator asks the question.

The participants in each sub-group respond simultaneously to Question 3.

The host at the table writes the responses on a Flip Chart.

Tools and support: Flip Chart.

Colored Felt-tip pens.

Sharing

Timing: 30 minute

What: While in a circle, everyone shares what she/he is grateful for and what she/he has learned.

Everyone answers the following questions:

*What have each of us learned for ourselves, about our projects, and for the entire group?

*What do we want to retain from the exchanges and tools that can be used when it comes to our own efforts? What am I grateful for? What are my next steps?

Who: The participants.

The facilitator

Ending of the Session
Timing: 5 minutes
What: The World Café is closed down.
Who: The facilitator

3.5 How Rigorously Should the Group's Time Be Managed?

One of the facilitator's roles is to rigorously (but not rigidly) monitor the rhythm and duration of the Mastermind group's processes. The use of a timer is a very effective way to make sure everyone sticks to the schedule. This respect for time is all the more important since each person comes to the Mastermind group so she/he can give and receive specific contributions.

It is especially important to maintain a consistent rhythm during the hot seat process. It is important to use a timer here for two essential reasons:

> Firstly, it allows people to express, in an equitable manner, her/his request for support from the group, and ensures each group member is able to go onto the hot seat, which is the main reason that each person has shown up.

> Then, there's a more subtle reason. Frequently, if there are no limits on time, the group's work has a tendency to spread itself out and turn into unproductive or futile debates. So everyone runs the risk that she/he will be wasting a lot of her/his time. Ideas don't necessarily need a long time to emerge. Under the proper conditions supporting collective intelligence, ideas can be almost immediately accessible. What is essential can be expressed in just a few minutes. There will be other opportunities for the members of the group during and outside of work meetings (lunches, break time, e-mails, phone calls, etc.), to spend more time resolving an issue, proposing a new idea and carrying out investigations, etc.

Thus, it is important that a Mastermind group facilitator keeps her/his eyes on the timer any time the group is involved in a process. It is a habit that should also be observed by the participants. If certain members of the group don't appreciate being "restricted" by an allotted amount of time, it might be useful to remind them of the pertinence of creative discipline, while confirming the need to maintain the right tempo.

Participants who complain about feeling too restricted by the kind of timing that is used during Mastermind group processes can be invited to also join other groups where they will be able to express themselves as much as they want to. Deciding to participate in a Mastermind group means that a person wants to make rapid progress. The dynamics that are generated by the rapid pace of the group processes are part of the learning. Some people may believe that restricting the time limits creativity. There are many examples, however, of projects that do not produce results no matter how much time is given. In Mastermind groups, the time restriction is intended to be a stimulus for taking action. And the large majority of ideas are there, just waiting to be expressed...

Therefore, the management of time is something that the facilitator needs to take care of. Participants who do not get their turn on the hot seat due to poor time management will understandable feel disrespected and "cheated"—it's akin to breaking a contract: When one shows up for a Mastermind group, going onto the hot seat is a top priority!

Between each Mastermind group process, it is important to spend a few moments on activities that are targeted at integrating and supporting group dynamics. They are useful so that each participant can remain fully attentive and be totally empowered. For example:

1. Going back to the COACH state. As Robert Dilts says: "You should never miss out on the opportunity to go back to the COACH state!" It is an excellent exercise to carry out if the group has any doubts or feelings of fatigue or boredom.

2. Jumping or running in place while listening to music (or not) to get rid of all of the tension that has come about because of concentrating hard, or because of being relatively immobile.

During a half-day spent in a Mastermind group, there is, generally speaking, enough time for 2 or 3 hot seat sessions, which last one hour apiece. Holding a series of them is nerve-racking, requires sustained attention, and taxes, to a very great degree, everyone's energy.

It is useful, in the time that remains, for the facilitator to vary the rhythm by proposing a different process, such a World Café, or by choosing another group processes among those that were described earlier. A facilitator may also want to propose "social" discussions or offer feedback about the experience of participants who went onto the hot seat at the time of the previous meeting, or about the influence of the meetings between participants, etc.

3.6 What is the Best Way for a Participant to Present their situation and Question to the Group?

As we have already pointed out, each Mastermindian, before she/he goes onto the hot seat, carefully prepares for it. The facilitator reminds her/him of it a few days before the session. She/He can request, in advance, descriptions of the different Mastermind group formats so that she/he can choose the one that is most appropriate for her/him.

The following is an example of a template that can be used to prepare a for the hot seat. Just as a reminder, a presentation to the group lasts a few or several minutes, depending on the time that the facilitator allocates to it. Priority is given to conciseness, in terms of the presentation and to getting "directly to the point".

I need to share:

1. My situation.

2. What I want to do or accomplish.

3. What I have already done or attempted.

4. What poses problems for me.

5. What I need.

6. What I expect from other Mastermindians.

3.7 So You Want to Start Your Own Mastermind Group

Although there are multiple possible formats (depending on the frequency and length of meetings) when it comes to running Mastermind groups, here we are going to study how to structure an approach that is spread out over a year, based on a model that is rather typical in the United States:

* 3 two-day long seminars.
* One webinar per month.
* Length of commitment: 1 year.

Our experience with collective intelligence shows that a real connection, every four weeks, is necessary for the energy, motivation, and good quality relationships to last.

Let's say that you are motivated and possess the skills necessary to lead a Mastermind group. You are, in all likelihood, an experienced coach or consultant and have an address book with lots of contacts in it. You have mobilized between four and seven participants so you can launch a Mastermind group. How does one organize what is supposed to take place over a year, and how should the first session be rolled out?

The first meeting is crucial; it is supposed to lay the foundations of a sustainable relational structure. It is a matter of sowing seeds of trust, of high quality relationships amongst members of the group, and of fostering a generative field. Although it is tempting to just attack business or leadership issues, it is better if you direct most of your attention at establishing a network of connections and the creation of a single focus. This field will allow the Mastermindians to start off on a path of transformation and to bring the treasures that everyone holds as part of their history to sessions so that they can be shared. Like in the case of bio-dynamic agriculture, the quality of the soil is everything.

The first meeting often serves as a measure of the strength of those who are with you. Pay attention to what does not happen—the effect from that could be devastating. The relational activities, the quality of the field that you create from the very first minutes in the group will determine, to a great extent, the success of a project.

Why Is "Formulating a Framework" the Highest Priority?

Mastermind groups first form and then develop. People are really infatuated nowadays with these collaborative approaches aimed at achieving success, but how many of them actually stick around for the duration? What are the basic ingredients that, if they are missing, make participants grow tired of Mastermind groups and lead them to drop out?

Answer 1: The absence of a framework.

Answer 2: Poor quality, when it comes the relationships that were created (see the following paragraphs).

Formulating the framework very early in the creation of a group is a basic condition that allows the group to continue. Not only formulating it, but repeating the formulation and making sure it is respected.

This framework will guarantee that there will be an "alliance" (as Napoleon Hill called it) between participants. To put it another way, it is a contract that connects the participants to one another and to the facilitator, and to the Mastermind spirit. Four concepts illustrate the idea of this kind of contract: 1) rules, 2) boundaries, 3) expectations, and 4) the sharing of responsibilities. They make up the steps that are laid out in establishing the Mastermind group contract.

To put it in concrete terms, when you recruit participants for your Mastermind group, you should make them aware of what it is they are committing themselves to. The following is an example of a Mastermind group contract:

Mastermind Group Contract

Rules

This contract is between (name of participant) and (name of facilitator), for a period of (weeks, months, quarters).

(Name of Mastermind group) is (definition of the MM group, and specific reason for its the existence). It shall bring participants together who identify themselves as having the following values: (values of the group).

(Name of the group) shall be made up of (number) participants. It shall meet on (days, dates, frequency) for (number of hours, at what times)... The place where meetings will occur shall be communicated to everyone before the group's first meeting.

(Number) webinars are planned during the member's participation. They shall last for (number of minutes) and shall take place on the third Thursday of the month, from 8:30 PM until 10 PM.

The recruitment of new participants   shall be carried out one/two/four times a year, in (month). Each member who is accepted into the group shall be unanimously approved by the group, after an interview with the facilitator.

The fee for participation in this group is (amount of fee), payable (number of times) at the beginning of every year. In the event of an absence, I will let (name of facilitator) know ahead of time, at (facilitator's phone number). I understand that fees will not be reimbursed, in full or in part, if I am absent from a session, or if my participation in the group is canceled. Plan your budget will be so you can make a monthly payment.

(Name of group) is not a business networking group, nor is it a career training or therapy group.

What is Expected of Members

Participating in this group requires adherence to the following basic terms and conditions:

That you commit to engage all (number) sessions that have been scheduled, or a significant percentage of those sessions. You commit to be in the service of the other participants' success (as defined by each of the participants), as much as your own, through your contacts, expertise, and every other kind of resource you have available to you. You commit to put these resources to good use for the group, at the same time taking care to respect each participant's responsibility in relation to achieving her/his own success.

Presence

You do hereby commit to making these meetings a top priority on your schedule. During a session, you will turn off your cell phone, not read or answer any e-mails, and will not disrupt it in any other way. In the event you cannot be physically present at the session, you can attend by SKYPE.

Participation

You do hereby commit to preparing for sessions and to actively participating in them, especially by going onto the hot seat.

Confidentiality

You do hereby commit to keep all information that will be shared in the group, either directly or indirectly, confidential, for all time, as well as information of either a personal or professional nature that is a part of the same. No recording of the sessions shall be permissible, other than when you are on the hot seat. You are permitted to take notes.

Personal Responsibility

You do hereby commit to taking responsibility for your professional situation and development. The group shall not be responsible for any consequences from actions you have or have not undertaken. Please leave your ego at the door before you come into the sessions.

If you don't fulfill these expectations, you authorize (name of the facilitator) to make decisions that will be in the best interests of the group. Keep in mind there will be no reimbursement for fees if you leave the group.

You commit to the following (example) etiquette:

* Be positive and encouraging when you challenge the other participants: i.e., caring without complacency.

* Arrive on time, and even in advance, if possible; finish on time. No one gets any additional time.

* The group addresses the professional, not personal aspects of things (except if the latter affects one's business activities).

* Have respect for different points of view. Make your own contribution and, at the same time, allow others to make theirs. You can criticize ideas, but don't criticize individual people. Stick to the issue and avoid private, off-to-the-side conversations.

* Avoid sensitive subject matter: i.e., religion, politics, sexuality.

* Don't hesitate to challenge the group's thinking—speak up when you don't agree.

* Respect your commitment to take action.

Facilitator's Responsibilities

The facilitator leads the group sessions. She/He is responsible for recruiting Mastermind group participants, making sure that the structure and rules of the group are respected, creating a safe place for everyone, managing the times for the group, making it go along with the planned agenda, giving feedback, seeing to it that the relational dynamics of the group are good, and supporting each participant when it comes to the implementation of her/his plan of action, during and between sessions.

Participant's Responsibilities

You agree to respect the terms and conditions of this contract.

To maintain the spirit of the group and its effectiveness, an evaluation shall be carried out every (number of weeks, months). These terms and conditions shall be re-defined once a year.

Signed at (place), on (date)

Participant's signature

Facilitator's signature

[Note that some Mastermind groups include in the contract a clause that addresses the exercise of confidentiality that is specific to their particular group.]

Why is the Creation of Relational Bonds the Second Most Important Priority for a Mastermind Group?

To share just how important the quality of relational bonds within a Mastermind group are, here is the testimony of a member who participated in a young Internet star's group.

> "At the end of the first Mastermind session, I took stock of what had taken place. A lot of ideas were exchanged. I attended some brilliant demonstrations that were carried out by highly successful speakers, including champions from the sports world. But I did not succeed in in establishing a "real" relationship with the facilitator. I created a tenuous bond with some of the participants. I didn't fill out the satisfaction survey that was handed out at the end of the meeting; that didn't upset the facilitator. What's more, he didn't talk to me about it. Finally, one of the participants, the only woman in the group, was ousted, without anyone knowing why, at the end of the first session. We learned why one month later, but in a way that had a mysterious ring to it, during a webinar. She wrote to me after the first session, in an attempt to find out why she was excluded: I didn't have an answer for that. That put me on guard."

We see, in this testimony, the seeds of an experience that turned out to be full of unfulfilled promises and quick dismissals. The creation of a relationship between the facilitator and each one of the participants, on the one hand, and between each member of the group, on the other, is key when it comes to sustainability, and, in all likelihood, when it comes to success. Placing emphasis on the relational aspect of the group, at the time of the initial session, needs to be the top priority.

The RSE of collective intelligence

One of the fundamental processes of team creativity is a simple one: It is what Robert Dilts calls the RSE of collective intelligence:

1. Resonance   **2. Synergies**   **3. Emergence**

Successfully achieving the first two steps above has a powerful effect. It leads to the emergence of collective intelligence. When there is resonance, people connect and get to know one another; they don't distance themselves from the things that they have in common. Taking the time to carry out this step is an investment that produces benefits long afterwards. Learning how to get to know one another and making use of relational and social intelligence are the keys that lead to success; people are not all that aware of them, and they aren't used all that much. Most of the time, people will pounce on the issues that have to do with business. Precesses for creating resonance need to be decided on, led, and kept alive; similar to what a musician does when she/he practices, on a regular basis, her/his musical scales. Without this first step, and without a framework, egos quickly confront one another, and the attitude of "may the best man win" prevails. In that case, little or no wisdom will come out of the group's exchanges. There is a risk that no one will come out of it with any growth whatsoever.

It is hardly a new discovery that the putting the foundations in place, are what are mostly determine just how solidly a building is constructed. The first session comes after the enthusiastic promises of the marketing initiative, and made at the time of the "recruitment" interview with the facilitator. This first session establishes what ingredients are going to make up this Mastermind group's specific "color". Some facilitators offer the opportunity for the new recruit to withdraw after the first session if it didn't live up to her/his one's expectations. People should be encouraged as much as possible to continue, however, because the great benefits that accrue from of a Mastermind group do so because of how long it goes on.

It is important to emphasize at this point that a candidate for a Mastermind group will also have to declare that she/he is open to being destabilized:

* Some of the things that she/he is sure about will be challenged.

* Some of her/his habits will be disrupted.

* Some of her/his choices will be challenged.

* Her/His choice of tools will be challenged.

* Some of her/his priorities will be challenged.

* Some of her/his strategies and techniques will be challenged.

* Her/His ego might just be disturbed!

When a person agrees to be challenged, it's that same thing as allowing herself/himself to carry out self-confrontation... She/He allows herself/himself to take in multiple points of view that come from outside of her/his comfort zone.

When group members use carefully phrased language that leads other participants to learn, because of a wealth of experience and wisdom, caring without complacency becomes a powerful resource in a Mastermind group.

Therefore, the priority for the first session is to create high quality relationships between participants. All of your talents as the initiator of the group, as well as its facilitator, should be put in the service of this priority.

You can be sure that all participants will be asking themselves the following questions, when they show up to a Mastermind group for the first time:

* Who are the other members in this group?

* Am I at the same level, or at a level that is below or above the others, in terms of success and social status?

* Does the facilitator feel concerned about my success?

* How will I experience and feel about going onto the hot seat in front of people whom I don't know?

The ability to create good quality relationships is, generally speaking, a key attribute that has been acquired by life coaches, trainers, and therapists who have learned to focus on the person with whom they are interacting. It is important for you to exercise that kind of sensitivity and empathy to get to the same point with the group. During the first meeting, when the foundations for groups are established, you lend it its tone. It is not a question of "business as usual". The Mastermind group should become a lasting point of reference for all participants. If you hold yourself back and don't throw yourself into supporting each Mastermindian in a committed way, don't use yourself in a way that allows them to climb up to the next step, and have no intention of encouraging them to make a quantum leap, what motivation will they still have after a few months?

Consider the experience, presented earlier, of a participant who was involved in a group cycle that lasted a year and was then forced out of the group. Since the facilitator did not feel "concerned" about his success, the participant thought that the return on the investment was not going to be enough. Tossing around some good ideas is just not enough. The Mastermind group is a space where support, comfort, and resources are supposed to be shared. This precondition is creation of a rich and supportive relationship especially with the facilitator, who bears responsibility for the group's progress. Secondly, it is important to remember that you, as a facilitator, are being paid for your efforts. The Mastermindians remain in the group, in particular because of the relationship that connects them with you, the facilitator.

If you want your Mastermind group to be a success, you will have to work hard at creating that relationship and offering support to each participant. That demonstrates your desire to hold to your initial promise: "I am going to help you go quickly up to the highest step, so you can rock the house and shatter the glass ceiling that has been holding you down for years." Whether explicit or implicit—explicit is more powerful when it comes to this matter—it is the promise that is made to each participant.

In his classic book *The Little Prince*, Antoine de Saint-Exupéry provides a poignant description of the importance of the creation of a bond in the following interaction between the Little Prince and the fox.

The Little Prince and the Fox

It was then that the fox appeared.

"Good morning," said the fox.

"Good morning," the little prince answered politely, though when he turned around he saw nothing.

"I'm here," the voice said, "under the apple tree."

"Who are you?" the little prince asked. "You're very pretty..."

"I'm a fox," the fox said.

"Come and play with me," the little prince proposed. "I'm feeling so sad."

"I can't play with you," the fox said. "I'm not tamed."

"Ah! Excuse me," said the little prince. But upon reflection he added, "What does 'tamed' mean?"

"You're not from around here," the fox said. "What are you looking for?"

"I'm looking for people," said the little prince. "What does 'tamed' mean?"

"People," said the fox, "have guns and they hunt. It's quite troublesome. And they also raise chickens. That's the only interesting thing about them. Are you looking for chickens?"

"No," said the little prince, "I'm looking for friends. What does 'tamed' mean?"

"It's something that's been too often neglected. It means, 'to create ties'..."

" 'To create ties'?"

"That's right," the fox said. "For me you're only a little boy just like a hundred thousand other little boys. And I have no need of you. And you have no need of me, either. For you I'm only a fox like a hundred thousand other foxes. But if you tame me, we'll need each other. You'll be the only boy in the world for me. I'll be the only fox in the world for you..."

(Taken from Richard Howard's translation)

This wonderful text, which is so well known, so little understood, so often forgotten about, and so little applied to one's life, should be taken as an ongoing inspiration for a facilitator who is starting a Mastermind group...

The importance of Making Use of the COACH State to Launch a Mastermind Group

The COACH state, which has been mentioned several times in this book, is an important resource to make use of at the time of a Mastermind group's launch.

This state is the foundation for groups that are able to work effectively using collective intelligence.

In big events led by popular motivational speakers, which sometimes bring together thousands of people, the focus is on stimulating motivation that could described as "extrinsic." The motivational guru might get people to jump about, shout over peppy music, break wooden planks under tons of applause, or carry out some other spectacular feat. The effect is guaranteed, senses are stimulated, and everyone feels overexcited and motivated. However, one has to wonder about the nature of and just how persistent this motivation is: Often, scarcely after the kind of event described above ends, the motivation "fizzles out" and then one goes back to what is her/his business as usual, and there is no long-lasting transformation...

In an effective Mastermind group, the COACH state is practiced as an ongoing discipline. Its power to bring people into a resourceful state frequently surprises people the first time they are exposed to it. In a Mastermind group seeking to maximize the collective intelligence of its participants, the shared COACH experience can cause a very powerful relational field to emerge

The opposite of the COACH state is the CRASH state; one in which people are tense and disconnected from themselves and each other. The following is a review the of the key characteristics of the COACH and CRASH states. [5]:

---

5   Reproduced with the kind permission of the author. Dilts, R., *Success Factor Modeling, Volume 2, Generative Collaboration, Releasing the Creative Power of Collective Intelligence*, published by Dilts Strategy Group, 2016.

# COACH	# CRASH
Generative State, being with	/ *Degenerative State, being against*

C - Centered	C - Contracted
0 - Open	R - Reactive
A - Alert	A - Analysis Paralysis
C - Connected	S - Separated
H - Hospitable	H - Hostile

No individual or group will be able to maintain a constant and consistent the COACH state. This is especially so when a group is first starting. It is easy for an individual or group to fall into a CRASH state without realizing it. It is a good discipline to periodically ask: At what point, on a scale of 0 to 10 (0 being CRASH, and 10 being COACH) are we? For a Mastermind group to work effectively we recommend that people are at 7 or above.

Fundamentally speaking, your role as facilitator is to lead the group into some form the COACH state and to try to keep people in that state as much as possible. You should pay attention to the group's ongoing state of mind and keep returning to the COACH state again and again, especially if the group seems to be headed in the direction of the CRASH state. It is best to focus your efforts in a way that is preventive by regularly having people check their overall state of mind. The COACH state has a great deal of influence on group dynamics and, thus, upon the quality of its actions and on results.

The speed with which a new Mastermind group will be able to act productively depends on the facilitator's ability to establish and increase the necessary level of trust. This will be accelerated by the group's ability to enter the COACH state. Once a good level of trust is established, you can bring in and use all of the other processes we have described. In a CRASH state, a group will struggle no matter what tools you use.

How Does One Start the First Session?

Let's imagine that eight people are participating in the launch of the Mastermind group that you have decided to lead in exchange for remuneration. Let's assume that this Mastermind group will meet in person two days, three times a year, and that there will be one webinar per month. The following is a suggestion for how one could allow it to unfold...

Arrival

The night before the start, the evening dinner is the first opportunity for informal sharing. This step is more important than it might seem. Every new group finds itself confronted with a great many issues, which can be conscious or unconscious. This initial, informal instance of sharing, in this case over a meal, is a way to establish the "creation of relationship" as the top priority. Before being a leader or a businesswoman/businessman, people are human beings. Sharing a meal creates, more than any other tradition, a kind of community, a unique type of field. It is preferable to locate a spot for his initial meeting that is rather tranquil, and where there is no kind of spectacle going on. Whether they know it or not, the Mastermindians are already having a session at this point. Their senses become sharper. Who is there? What is the facilitator's attitude? How do I feel when I'm around these people whom I don't know? Am I where I should be? Have I done the right thing by starting off on this venture ?, etc. The attention that you, as the facilitator, pay to each person, creates the rhythm for the relationships that are going to be created... or not.

The First Morning: Facilitator's Introduction

Particular attention needs to be paid to the facilitator's introduction. Everyone is anxious to get started. They got an initial impression at the dinner the night before. How did each of them who were in that group feel? Personal speculations combine with curiosity about the new experience.

Quite obviously, the timetable for launching the group should be carefully respected. 8:30 on the dot, for example.

This time is crucial because it allows you to set the tone for what will follow. The time when the group was launched will remain recorded in the participants' memory forever. The first words that are chosen, the first looks, the pace that is proposed, the priorities that are felt or expressed determine the foundation for building on the group.

The following are some examples of possible ways to start a Mastermind group. They are just suggestions to stimulate your own creativity during this crucial time in your group's formation.

""Good, it's time... We're going to start. I'm going to share with you what's going to happen, but first, I want to introduce myself..."

By saying something like:

"In the first letter that the philosopher Seneca sent to Lucilius during the 1st Century AD, he stated: 'The most shameful kind of loss is the one we incur through negligence. And if you think about it, a great part of life wastes away in Evil, a greater yet in doing just nothing at all. All of that amounts to doing something other than what we should!'"

Or else:

"Do you know what was the first thing that Steve Jobs did when he had a new idea, or when he came up with a creative suggestion? He would quietly begin to share it with 100 people explore their thoughts, ideas and reactions..."

Or else:

"Three years ago, my sales were down by 50%. My professional situation was so precarious that I went through a phase where I was terribly anxious. I then had the chance to find... to make the following decision... to finally implement this suggestion that I..."

You get the idea. It's the principle of "story telling". Start with an anecdote by reading an inspiring text, or one that puts forth a main idea. One has to captivate the group's imagination immediately, through references to the philosophical or business world, or by drawing from one's own experiences. Many facilitators do not adequately prepare for this key moment. How many groups start up with an intention that is not fully energized? "Intensity" is the key word when it comes to being a good facilitator.

The Second Essential Theme: The Mastermind Group's Goal

After your introductory comments, you remind everyone of the raison d'être for your Mastermind group – why you have created this very special group, what your intention for the participants is and what you, basically speaking, are facilitating. Overall, a Mastermind group's goals should be high-level and ambitious. Whatever the goals of each individual present (they often have to do with their businesses, raising their social status, or the pursuit of a strong social leadership, or an environmental goal), you should announce your strong commitment to promoting everyone's success; you should encourage everyone to take the biggest step, and even beyond. Your goal as a facilitator, at this point, is to give participants direction. You want participants to be as clear and enthusiastic as possible.

The impact of words, particularly when it comes to establishing the foundation of the group, is decisive. Facilitators are sometimes insufficiently aware of the very first words they say. Consider the care you would take, when writing the introduction or conclusion to an important paper or article. The clarity and effectiveness of the words you choose at the beginning will set the tone and direction for what follows.

Then comes the presentation of the path the group will follow. Without getting into too many details, this exercise is necessary to make your presence in the group legitimate. Your credibility, training and experience should make Mastermindians feel that they have come to a good place. Even before finding out about the backgrounds and skills of the others "in the room", every participant will need to feel that the facilitator is in possession of something that is significant and valuable for the whole group.

Introductions Around the Table

Another important step of launching a Mastermind group is that of going around the table so that everyone can introduce themselves. That moment is a delicate one... It can be tempting at this stage to propose an activity where everyone would be forced to come out of her/his comfort zone. However, the main priority is that of creating strong and safe relationship. We propose a format involving simply going around the table slowly and offering five minutes to each person to share the following information (no timer at this stage).

* Who I am, my family, professional background ...

* Why I chose to participate in this Mastermind group. What are my expectations ...

* What I think I can bring to this group ...

* What am I passionate and enthusiastic about ...

This format allows space for each person to share something meaningful. One shouldn't go too fast, and one should allow some time for different personalities to express themselves. Experienced facilitators may tempted to use some of their favorite tricks such as ice breakers, mutual introduction techniques and other rapport building tactics—But that is not necessarily helpful or desirable during this first stage.

Instead, while going around the table, with everyone speaking in turn, in no particular order, you will want to write the ideas that emerge, and which seem important to you, on the board. In particular, people's expectations and what each person thinks she/he can contribute to the group. That allows you, at the end of the activity, to check and see if those expectations correspond to what you intended planned to put on the menu. If necessary, you can, as a consequence, adjust the activities you are offering.

As a facilitator, you will want to have a variety of possible questions to choose from which will allow each participants to go more deeply into what they are sharing, such as the following:

* What I like about life.

* An initiative I took, an adventure I experienced, and of which I am proud.

* My favorite hobbies.

* My 3 greatest successes.

* My 3 greatest failures, and the lessons I learned from them.

* Etc.

As an alternative to this first round of "going around the table" you can try an RSE (Resonance/Synergy/Emergence) activity such as the following:

Ask participants to prepare responses to a few questions before they come to the session, so that they can be written quickly, by each of them, on a flip chart sheet. You ask for all of the sheets so you can make a square or a rectangle with them, to be put on the wall (using something adhesive). Make sure that the sheets touch one another (otherwise, you'll get marks on the wall). Each person will draw, with crayons or a colored felt tip pen, lines from her/his group of words to those on the other sheets that resemble them (that is to say, she/he moves in the direction of the resonances she/he has with the other participants), and draws a circle around the differences (these are potential synergies).

Then each person expresses what the pattern of lines and circles evokes in her/him, that is to say, what it has caused to come into her/his mind (i.e., what has emerged). By this point, you have already carried out the fundamental collective intelligence sequence: Resonance – Synergy – Emergence.

Following the introduction is a good time to take a break.

Collective Intelligence Activity

After the break, you may want to do something like read the excerpt from *The Little Prince*, shared a few pages ago, or some other text that emphasizes the importance of creating relationship.

This is often a good moment to propose a collective intelligence activity. Consider, for example, the fox's proposal to the little prince: *"First you'll sit down a little ways away from me, over there, in the grass. I'll watch you out of the corner of my eye, and you won't say anything".* Invite the participants to not say anything at first. Observe one another for a while. Then slowly and silently draw close to one another so "the fox can be tamed." A simple bonding activity like this can be done in just a few minutes.

We suggest something like this in place of many typical quick, but potentially superficial, rapport building techniques.

The COACH state Experience

The upshot of all of this is that there is an opportunity to deepen the quality of relationships and the generative field among Mastermind group participants. Rather than through a lot of cognitive activity, this is better achieved through the creation of a collective COACH state experience.

Let's make a small detour by citing a metaphor written by Eckhart Tolle: *"Imagine that you are in a nightclub in the middle of a forest. The music is so powerful that it seems to find its way into every pore of your body. You have to shout to communicate. The light is sometimes weak, sometimes very lively and colorful. You can smell things of every kind: perfume, alcohol, and sweat... Every one of your senses is bombarded.*

Needing to get some air, you go out of the discotheque and find that you are smack dab in the middle of the forest. The darkness and silence, instantaneously, make you feel somewhat soothed and relaxed.

However, you, very quickly, become bored. Next to the hail of light, sound, and all of the smells in the nightclub, the forest is a spectacle that is not all that captivating.

However, after a moment, something special happens: Your senses open up slowly to the environment. You pick up on little animal sounds, the rustling of leaves, your sense of smell captures the subtle perfume of the wet earth and plants, your eyes begin to make out shapes, movements, and the flickering of moonlight between branches. Little by little, you feel won over by the feeling of being in a sacred place that surrounds and embraces you. And you understand that this place is simply Life. It is a flow of vibrations, which can be either powerful or delicate, which flows through everything, that is to say, through all places and throughout time, but which, in the nightclub, you won't pick up on.

You become overtaken by emotion that cannot be described, which might seem a lot less spectacular than that caused by what goes on in the nightclub. But it is infinitely more profound and sustaining: You are in peace."

Getting into what is referred to as the "COACH state" comes about from the stimulation of intrinsic motivation; that is, one goes and searches inside for that special, unique dimension that is not induced by the environment or the beliefs of others. At the time of the Mastermind group's first foray into the "COACH state", participants are invited to share what will change this team into a crucial instrument of transformation for each one of them.

The Initial Hot Seat Session

Once sufficient rapport is established, it is the moment for the first person to go onto the hot seat. It's probably a good idea to start this process without revealing any details about it, and just let people get the experience. It is similar to teaching a person a new card game. If someone tries to explain all the rules at the beginning, the person becomes lost. Putting theory before experience is often a mistake. This bias, found in a lot of traditional education, often leaves high quality students at a disadvantage. It does, however, turn out to be useful to introduce the process in a theoretical manner at the end of this initial session, using a chart that outlines the synthesis at work. That allows everyone to get used to it.

It is often useful to end the first morning with another hot seat session.

Passing the "Talking stick" to Allow Someone to Speak

The "talking stick" is a tool developed by Native Americans to help promote collective intelligence. It can be very helpful when participants are sharing or reflecting on their experience. The basic principle is for the speaker to hold onto a baton or some other light object while she/he is talking. When that person is finished, the object is placed in the middle of the group or passed on to whomever the one who has been doing the talking chooses; preferably not the person next to her/him. This piece of equipment creates conditions that are conducive to improved listening, on the part of the others, and allows the group to avoid the scenario where everyone would be talking over everybody else. The use of a baton also strengthens each person's awareness that she/he is a member of a group. It is also an easy way of keeping track of who has and has not spoken...

Lunchtime

The First Afternoon: Recreational or Nature Activity (1 hour)

As every experienced facilitator knows, it is a good idea to plan to do something physical and energizing right after lunch. If you don't, the fatigue that comes about from the process of digestion will inevitably spread through most of the group.

Therefore, after lunch is often a good time for a recreational activity, or better yet, for spending an hour "surrounded by nature". A Mastermind group is a rare opportunity to connect with one's project in a powerful way. It is also an excellent time to get back in touch with oneself. After lunch, a walk, in a smaller group, each of which has its own theme for discussion, or alone, which doesn't necessarily have to have any particular direction, can be thought of as space and time for people to recharge their energy.

Two Hot Seat Sessions

Once everyone goes back to the room, the afternoon might be organized as follows:

* One hot seat session.

* A special topic which would be useful to the group that you have chosen as the facilitator

* A second hot seat session.

What is Achieved in the First Day

It is often a good idea to complete the first day of a Mastermind group by taking turns to reflect, using the talking stick, allowing each person to share...

* What she/he has retained from what went on.

* What she/he has particularly appreciated.

* What upset her/him.

* Why certain decisions that were made before should be dropped.

The goal is to end the first day by 7 PM.

Relaxing Recreational/Touristic Activities in the Evening

It is a good idea to plan for a relaxing evening. Instead of going through an exhausting marathon of nighttime activities, you should come up with relaxing activities, such as a light meal, and if possible, depending where the group is being held, a visit to a nearby tourist attraction, etc.

All the bonds that are created at those times will make up the substance of the group. Participants will derive pleasure from mutual exploration and discovery. The group will thrive from the development of each of its members.

There should be no shortage of these opportunities during the course of a Mastermind group.

The Second Day

The second day of a beginning Mastermind group session will greatly resemble the first. Keep in mind that everyone needs to go onto the hot seat. Four sessions will need to be scheduled for each day.

As the group begins to take shape it will be necessary to plan one session for the clarification and adjustment of the rules, so that the group can function the way it's supposed to. You will also need to go over the meeting dates for the coming year.

During this session, all participants should be made aware of the following things:

* The group's rules of confidentiality.

* The caring without complacency principle.

* The entry and exit processes for participants.

* The direction and goal of the Mastermind group.

* The necessary mindset for effective participation.

* The ground rules that have to be respected.

* The kind of attitudes that can lead to exclusion from the group.

* How one is supposed to go on the hot seat.

The hot seat isn't the only essential thing that one finds in a Mastermind group. The collective mindset of the group is crucial. As a result, the first session basically includes establishing that mindset, which involves each person who is present. The Mastermind group is not a training group; nor is it a conference. It reflects a sincere decision to change; it is where each person becomes much more than just an actor... She/He is the actual creator of her/his own transformation. Each person comes with a strong motivation to take action and to not to remain nothing more than a spectator of others' successes or genius. Each of the participants brings in her/his own resources. The experience on the hot seat turns out to be revealing, and the group contributes its support the whole time that it is going on.

The facilitator can insert activities that will allow for the strengthening of relationships between hot seat sessions. For example:

"I see, I sense, and I like that" (usually done in a group of 5 people)[6]. This is powerful processes that creates bonds between people who do not know one another. The participants sit in a circle and each person takes turns being person "A" (when she/he is the other members' center of the group's attention). One at a time, each of the other participants says to A, "When I look at you, here is what I see: ...., here is what I sense........, and I like that." It is an activity than can take some time because it is necessary to allow each person enough time to let their perceptions emerge. However, it is a good investment in terms of developing a good quality of relationship. The positive feedback from fellow participants will, in all likelihood, will have a resounding effect on the person who is receiving it.

It is also important, as far as the group experience is concerned, to make an inventory of all of the themes that might promote the development of each person. Do the group members need to address business management, marketing, technological, personal organization or financial issues, for example? In effect, you are preparing for upcoming meetings as you explore those needs. Although the first session is unique in its focus (priority is given to the creation of the group, relationships, and the hot seat experience), the meetings that come after will enrich new activities, interventions that have a high added value, and organized activities that make progress possible.

The first session ends by going around the table and having each member share her/his impression and what she/he has learned and discovered. It is also an opportunity for members to get support from the rest of the group for three commitments to action. The facilitator should record each Mastermindian's three points and encourage the entire group to support

---

6   Dilts, Robert, Formation de facilitateur en intelligence collective, in conjunction with the Evolution et Synergie agency, Avignon, 2015. Reproduced with the kind permission of the author.

the commitment to take action. Rather than looking at this commitment as something that is rigid or restrictive, it should be seen as an opportunity for each individual to make her or his next steps public and receive the support of the group to achieve them. It is well known that commitments that are expressed, written, or announced have a greater chance of being carried out than those tucked away, deep inside, in the form of nothing more than good resolutions...

What Is the Role of the Facilitator at the Time of the First Session?

The position of facilitator is neither that of a coach nor a trainer. It falls somewhere in between. On one hand, the facilitator acts as a leader, guaranteeing that the process will unfold in such a way to maximize the collective intelligence of the group. On the other hand, she/He tries to stay in the background, giving maximum space to the participants, the development of their projects and business, and the emergence of different, varied collaborations among the group members. The facilitator offers her/his opinion while the hot seat sessions are going on, but does so without dominating the situation.

What Takes Place at the Second Session (and the Following Ones)?

The dynamics are different at the time of the launch of the second Mastermind session. The group will already be formed, and some exchanges will have taken place through e-mails, phone conversations and webinars (see the paragraph that addresses this further on) since the first meeting, Specific expectations will have been identified. Thus, the second session is structured as follows:

* Welcome and social time.

* Establishment of the collective mindset (COACH state).

* Feedback.

* Going over what has happened since the last time.

* Identification of the biggest problems and successes.

* Identification of how the Mastermind group is going to start to influence the success of projects that are going on.

* Feedback from the Johnny's who were on the hot seat during the previous meeting.

* Hot seat sessions.

* Special sessions or interventions by experts.

* Identification of commitments to be carried out between now and the next meeting.

* Circle where the meeting is closed.

It should be emphasized that some new participants might end up joining the group after the initial gathering has taken place. Therefore, it's up to you to plan, in a systematic way, how you will call on the on the spirit that governs this experience, and to set aside a specific time so that new arrivals will find a place where they can introduce and express themselves.

Welcome/Social Time

A Mastermind group is a social one. Its effectiveness depends on the quality of relationships between the members. A welcoming and social environment is essential to the group's success. Each individual participant needs to take time for exchanges with her/his co-Mastermindians about matters of her/his choosing. A sufficient but not excessive amount of time, so that it doesn't impinge on that set aside for the "productive" group processes, needs to be set aside for that.

Feedback

It's useful for each Johnny to present feedback about what he has implemented after going onto the hot seat. This feedback has several functions:

* It incites Johnny to actually take action since he knows that he will have to share what he has done after he went onto the hot seat.

* It allows the members to find out if Johnny is making progress as a result of participating in the group (this is also an important clarification for Johnny himself).

* It allows each Mastermindian to evaluate the pertinence and effectiveness of the elements he contributed at the time of the previous meeting. Group members are always pleased when they notice that their ideas and proposals have allowed a Johnny to make progress or draw closer to her/his goal. Making progress together. cements the bonds between the members of a group.

Going On the Hot Seat

This entire book could be summed up as being a teaching tool for facilitators who lead hot seat sessions. That process is, in effect, the heart of a Mastermind group – the difference that makes the difference, the reason the group exists. Every person who has an authentic desire to make progress and who has undergone a session on the hot seat is actually eager to go through the experience again, and on a regular basis. That is the very reason why people sign up for a Mastermind group.

Each work session that takes place inside of a Mastermind group includes, at its very core, having every one of the participants go onto the hot seat.

Special Sessions

You can offer other sessions to the group, or interventions by experts who address themes that have emerged as a result of expressed or induced expectations. Make sure that the contributions that have been offered as a model of success, as interventions by outside experts, or the other processes you have chosen to employ, add an undeniable value to the group for participants.

Commitments Start with the First Meeting and Continue into the Next

The affirmation of commitments, in front of the group, to actively pursue the goal of success (which was mentioned above) is a powerful group process. People often find it is easy to "make good resolutions" but often find it challenging to follow through with them. On the other hand, when a member of a group makes the commitment, in front of everyone else, that she/he will undertake certain, specific actions, what then goes on in the group becomes a lot more stimulating, and all participants experience an intrinsic kind of motivation. For example, you can ask each participant to write her/his three commitments and the three major decisions she/he has made on a flip chart sheet. What is written on that sheet will be used at the beginning of the next meeting. You can film a short video during which each person shares, in 30 seconds, her/his three key points. Afterwards, the video is shared on the web space that has been reserved for the group.

Is it necessary to demand that a participant make a commitment? It may seem like only a small detour in the group's activity. To some, it can also feel like a burden ... In fact, once, when a facilitator was going around the table and addressing the subject of commitment, one of the participants declared her opposition: "I feel like I'm re-living something from the time of Communist Eastern Europe!" The facilitator's response was such that it calmed her reaction, which was understandable since it came from someone who had lived behind the Iron Curtain: "If you change the word 'commitment' to 'desire' or 'intention', does that resonate better with you?"

It is important to welcome the reaction of a Mastermindian who does not want to commit to acting on things. What purpose does it serve to force a doubtful, reticent participant, who feels blocked, to take action? However, if a participant does not express herself/himself at this crucial time—a necessary condition for taking action—it is worth asking her/him, in a private conversation, about what she/he is looking for from being in a Mastermind group. Remaining a spectator does not serve the individual in question or the group. If a participant does not want to make commitment, it is in her/his own best interests, and those of the group, to head out the door. There needs to be at least some small indications that the person has a desire to change.

It is frequently helpful to ask group members, "What commitment (desire, intention) are you taking up here that you wouldn't have if you hadn't become a part of this group?" This question demonstrates to the group members that it's because of their Mastermind group participation that they get really good ideas, support and that they are able to implement ideas quickly.

How Should Sessions End?

When ending a session it is important to check to see if some participants have the need for some kind of special support. This could include a phone call, an extra session between regular meetings, or coaching. It is also crucial to create a bridge to the next session and to formalize, along with the everything else, the goals for the next meeting. Everyone is then thanked, and the unique scope of the session is highlighted.

The closing circle is an important moment. It is often not done properly because of a lack of time. Nevertheless, it is the chance to settle things, feel anchored, and reflect on individual and collective contributions, from which everyone has benefited. It is also an opportunity to show appreciation to other members of the group for how they helped to bring about progress, and for the ideas they shared. Each person expresses how she/he feels, what she/he retains from her/his participation and what is in her/his heart. Be sure you set aside enough time to focus on this important moment of solidarity, gratitude, and recognition for the work that has been accomplished.

Each participant will now be able to go about his/her business, carry out her/his projects in an active fashion, make things to happen, shatter the glass ceiling, climb up to the next level, and enthusiastically wait for the next Mastermind session.

How Do Participants Meet Up Between Sessions? Through the Hosting of Webinars?

Why Webinars Are Arranged

If the Mastermind model that has been proposed in this chapter is used, three two-day seminars, spread out over a year, take place, with eight participants. Each face-to-face meeting is very intense. Nevertheless, the period of time between each of those meetings distances the Mastermindians from the group's spirit, their engagements with one another, and the energy they have created together.

The webinar (a meeting on the Internet using a camera and the sharing of a screen) allows Mastermindians to maintain connections on a regular basis, in spite of the distance that separates them. By having regular virtual meetings, a feeling of belonging is reinforced, positive bonds and stimulating interactions are re-activated and mutual engagement resurfaces. Everybody can see one another again, and share and attach documents in real time. In brief, everyone can have almost the same experience that she/he has had during face-to-face meetings; although interpersonal exchanges on the Internet will never replace the power of in-person encounters.

What Takes Place during a Webinar?

The webinar takes place during a very short amount of time. It is used so that interpersonal bonds can be maintained and so that the group can continue to be led to the point where they will have access to the highest level. Therefore, it's an additional opportunity for organizing quicker and quicker hot seat sessions of the Johnny bombing type, which we looked at earlier.

Recommendations for Web Hosting:

* Quick welcome and introduction by the host.

* Guiding the group to the COACH state.

* Reminder of the rules of the game: length of the meeting, muting of the microphone, raising one's hand or pushing the web tool's "raise hand" button to start talking, etc.

* Agenda for the group.

* Personal forecast: a quick turn where each person shares key information. The Johnny's from the previous session give feedback and indicate what progress they have made.

* Two or three participants, who have expressed a previous desire, go onto the hot seat.

* Schedule for upcoming events.

* Closing with a new personal forecast.

What Are the Basic Rules for Hosting a Webinar?

Participating in webinars requires some learning, first on the part of host, and then on that of the members. It is different than working together in person. Some things should be looked out for, and rules need to be respected:

* The meeting time should be chosen in a way that is agreeable to everyone, in particular, if the different Mastermindians do not live in the same time zone.

* The start and end times of the session need to be respected.

* Each person should be able to make herself/himself comfortable, in an environment that is calm.

* Each person should be able to express herself/himself. It is up to the host to make sure that that takes place, including by using a timer.

* Each person should mute her/his microphone when she/he is not talking so that there is no confusion of voices.

* If someone wants to express herself/himself, it is appropriate and more efficient for her/him to "raise her/his hand."

The webinar can be recorded; that creates a double advantage: The participants can listen to it all over again, and those who did not attend can take advantage of it at a later time.

How Long Should the Webinar Last?

The webinar should last for a relatively short period of time. Experience shows that it is more difficult for people to maintain sustained attention online than when they are face-to-face with others. Two hours seems to be good, possibly three when there is a 10-minute break at the mid-point of the session. It is better to have more sessions scheduled (for example, one or two webinars per month) than to have just one long one. Moreover, two-hour webinars are easier to fit into people's schedules.

Why does Verbal Activity Need to be Monitored during a Webinar?

To promote collective intelligence, each person in group needs to be able to express herself/himself freely. The hosting of a webinar, however, requires special monitoring. There are several reasons for that:

* Participation in Internet meetings is a practice that has barely begun, and is even unknown to a lot of people.

* Verbal exchanges during a web meeting don't have the same dynamics as those that take place in person.

* The host cannot control outside interference found in each participant's environment.

The "chat" function allows, for those who want it, the ability to send messages during the meeting. It is a tool that one should use because it is very practical: One participant can share a web address that somebody has just talked about, add smiley faces to encourage those who are expressing themselves, or start a private chat to ask for an opinion or a clarification from only one other person.

Monitoring of the webinar is necessary for it to be effective, and for each participant to really benefit (from shared ideas and energy) from it.

Is the Use of Webinars Unavoidable?

In this chapter, we have described the hosting of a Mastermind group, orchestrated around three two-day seminars, and carried out over a period of a year. That kind of tempo usually turns out to not be adequate for relationships between group members to grow strong, and for progress to become tangible. If the group's participants are at some distance from one another, geographically speaking, the use of webinars is unavoidable. Even if they are in close proximity to one another, the flexibility of webinars makes meetings easier for everyone, including at hours "outside of the norm" (in the evening, at lunchtime, on the weekend).

There are now a lot of tools available which allow one to work online efficiently. Why deprive yourself of them? They can often lead to the development of intense relationships without having to physically go to where the others are, which is costly in terms of time and energy.

Are You Ready to Launch Your Group?

The goal of this chapter was to help you understand how a complete Mastermind group cycle unfolds. It is an overview for how to facilitate such a group. All that remains is to verify that you are indeed motivated to be a facilitator, that you will carry out all of the marketing efforts that you need to promote your Mastermind group, and that you will take action... Participating yourself in one or several Mastermind groups, adapting yourself to their methods, drawing inspiration from recommendations that emerge from collective intelligence, are helpful prerequisites for forming your own group. But more than anything else, you need to take the chance and get started.

Do you feel ready ?

Chapter 4

How Does a Facilitator Create and Organize a Mastermind Group?

When a facilitator thinks about creating a Mastermind group, she/he has to take the four following dimensions into account: (1) She/He, of course, begins by preparing herself/himself because she/he will be the main influence on the group's success. This issue was presented in the second part of the book. (2) Attention will also be paid to logistical preparation for the group, (3) preparation for the overall process, that is to say, the facilitation and supportl of the group's dynamics, and finally, (4) to the preparation for each meeting.

4.1 Preparation for the Overall Process

To prepare for a Mastermind group, the facilitator must ask herself/himself a certain number of questions. The following are some that she/he must answer before she/he can actually create and offer a Mastermind group to others:

* Am I going to require a fee for participation in my Mastermind group, or is it going to be free?

* Will sessions be face-to-face, online, or both?

* What will the frequency and length of sessions be?

* Where will it take place, and how will I manage all of the logistics?

* How will I make people feel like they want to participate in it?

* How will I let people find out about my Mastermind group?

* What kinds of processes will I offer to participants?

* How will I bring new people into the group?

* How will I be able to raise the level of my Mastermind group?

* What kinds of organized activities will I offer between face-to-face sessions?

* Should meetings have a specific theme?

* How will I evaluate participants' satisfaction with the group?

The facilitator also has to reflect on her/his Mastermind group's overall process. What kind of facilitation should she/he implement, as a function of the kind of participants that she/he has enrolled in the venture, based on their desires and stated ambitions? What kind of processes is she/he going to implement that will serve them? She/He asks herself/himself, more than anything else, about how she/he is going to initiate the dynamics of collective intelligence in the group, and bring about an emergence of ideas that will make the Mastermindians say "Wow!"

Some facilitators prepare the exact content that they are going to use during meetings ahead of time. However, that may not be the best course of action. It is difficult to know exactly what Johnny is going to ask the group. The facilitator will have to be very flexible when it comes to the activities and workshops that she/he will offer, since it depends on the questions that are put forth by participants. She/He must always be ready to listen, and constantly in "meta mode", that is to say, both fully present and an observer, with "one foot in, and one foot out", to understand what is at stake at any given time. She/he must be able to plan organized activities, at the same time that she/he knows that things will surely take place differently than she/he has planned. The facilitator constantly adjusts her/his proposal for the organized activities based on the needs of the participants and, in particular, for the person who is going to go on the hot seat.

Descriptive Matrix

The following descriptive matrix will allow the facilitator of the Mastermind group to clarify her/his ideas as she/he comes up with them. It will help her/him ask herself/himself some good questions about those ideas as soon as she/he begins to reflect on them. This matrix, in particular, will allow her/him to draw up, afterwards, a questionnaire that will be targeted to the recruitment of group members. The following is an example of a descriptive matrix that the creator of a Mastermind group might fill out:

Matrix for a Mastermind Group

Name of the Mastermind Group:

Status (Is it a group that's already in existence, or is it one that's in the process of being created?):

Targeted Public:

Group Size:

Minimum Number of Participants:

Maximum Number of Participants:

The Group's Intention:

The group's goal is...

Minimum Length of Commitment:

Pace and Frequency of Meetings:

Kind of Meetings:

Number of Face-to-Face Meetings:

Number of Online Meetings:

Acceptance Method that Will Be Used for Candidates:

Initial Candidates:

Candidates Who Join Later:

Cost of Sessions:

4.2 Sending of Invitations and Preparation of a Schedule

Even if all of the Mastermindians have perfect knowledge of the date of the next meeting, the facilitator sends them an invitation, through e-mail messaging, a few days ahead of time as a reminder of the time and place for it. At that time, she/he asks each of the participants if she/he would like to go on the hot seat, in which case, those Mastermindians, in particular, are supposed to prepare for it. This question is important because one should carefully prepare for the hot seat. The meetings, generally speaking, are short, so time shouldn't be wasted at the beginning of a session trying to figure out who is going to be on the hot seat or whether Johnny's situation and question are clear, complete, and pertinent. Therefore, part of the preparation for the meeting will consist, for the facilitator, of gathering information about participants' issues and questions, and of making sure that the Johnny who is about to go onto the hot seat, or future Johnny's, are properly prepared.

The facilitator also asks Johnnys who have recently gone on the hot seat to prepare some feedback that will explain the actions they have taken, and to describe the results of the same. These feedback sessions are sources of collective enrichment and make the members feel united, especially if the results that have been achieved are good.

The facilitator prepares the schedule based on the number of Mastermindians that she/he thinks will be going onto the hot seat and any other processes or sessions she/he might want to carry out. Also, a Mastermindian might request time so that she/he can make a point with the others about an important issue. Time might also be set aside for an intervention by an expert or witness.

If no Mastermindian asks to go on the hot seat (which would be a bad sign, in terms of group dynamics), the facilitator will come up with generic training sessions, such as:

* How to make full use of the people in your network and address book.
* How to manage situations that are emotionally difficult.
* How to define ambitious goals.
* How to increase the level of your personal and collective ambitions.
* How to manage your time better.
* How to make decisions when you are in the middle of a complicated situation.
* Etc.

Example of an Invitation: Sent Five to Seven Days
before a Follow-Up Session

Hello Everyone,

I hope everything is going well, that you are full of energy, and that your projects are off to a really good start…

We are going to have the pleasure of meeting again, for our next Mastermind group, on …………

This session will take place in the auditorium of the Manor of the dragonflies… (See the attached map—That will show you how to get in).

We will meet there between 8:30 AM and 5:30 PM.

You all know how important it is to arrive on time to our meetings.

Each one of you should let me know before ………… (5 or 6 days before the meeting) if you want to be on the hot seat so that I can come up with the right schedule for this meeting.

Come with your answers to the following questions:

* What is it you want to do and succeed at, at this point?

* What project do you want to move forward on?

* What concerns or problems do you want to resolve for yourself?

Kind Regards,/

The Facilitator

A second invitation is sent out two or three days
before the meeting:

Hello Everyone,

I hope everything is going well for you.

I have the pleasure of sending the schedule for our meeting on… which will take place at Manor of the dragonflies

Jeff has asked to go onto the hot seat regarding a business opportunity, and Céline, so she can get some ideas about how she can improve her communication skills.

Nadia will tell us about the promotion of her book on participatory management.

Finally, Laurent will submit, to the group, a project that has to do with the service center that he and his wife want to set up.

I would also like us to spend 30 minutes talking about the two-day seminar that is going to take place in Aspen, Colorado, in July, where one of those days will be set aside hiking and reflection.

As was decided the last time we met, we will eat in the manor's restaurant.

Please get in touch with me right away in the event that any of you have any issue with any of the above.

Kind Regards,

The Facilitator

(cell phone number)

The invitations should be taken seriously. It's better to avoid any pleasantries and rough guesses about anything that will be taking place. The invitations should remind participants of the reason for the group, which often addresses (but not necessarily) issues that have to do with business or a change in the level of members' success.

Invitation Sent to a New Participant

When the facilitator invites someone to participate in the group for the first time, the message he sends might be a bit different than the one above. Here is an example:

Dear Theo/Amandine,

I am very happy at the thought of welcoming you into the Mastermind group. I am sure that you will contribute a great deal, which will enhance its value for everyone.

I am also sure that you will benefit a lot from your participation, make progress with your projects, and give concrete expression to your ambitious goals.

The first meeting will be held on ...., at Manoir des Libellules.

The purpose of this first meeting is to ....

We will get to know one another, and you will share your intentions and goals with us.

On behalf of the group, I invite you to take part on the day indicated above. At that time, you will be able to get a good idea of how our Mastermind group functions. After that, we will be able to make plans for you to join, if it seems that it will be in everybody's best interests.

Best Regards,

The Facilitator

4.3 How Long Does a Mastermind Group Remain in Existence?

Does a Mastermind group have a pre-programmed, time-limited existence? We don't think that it should. As long as the participants find it relevant, they will continue to come to the meetings and the group will go on for a long time. A Mastermind group is a living unit that needs only one thing to last: a person who sends out invitations. Some Mastermind groups have lasted for scores of years. However, no one wants to a-priori commit to several years of an activity without knowing what benefit she/ he is going to get from it. Therefore, it is better to not make prospective members sign a contract before trying session. A one-year commitment is typical for a Mastermind group. The initial commitment can, however, cover a shorter period of time, for example two or three meetings, so that the candidate can size up her/his level of commitment, and so that the facilitator can gauge the candidate's the compatibility with the group that she/he is leading.

This commitment is certainly the initial impetus; but after that, it can turn, more than anything else, into a deeply-felt dynamic, one of internal, long-lasting motivation. The facilitator will have to keep this motivation alive through the quality of the interaction, and by using a framework that will give Mastermindians the desire to continue to make progress together, in a way that is strong and quick. It is necessary for participants to make a long-term commitment to actively participate in the group experience, and in its dynamic unfolding, so that all participants can be served. The longer the group lasts, the greater the benefits will generally be that come about from it.

A facilitator can, of course, put a limit on the period of time that her/ his Mastermind group is going to last; but that seems, to us, like a strange thing to do, because the benefits that come about from a Mastermind group make themselves felt, more and more, the longer it continues. If the Mastermindians are happy, why not continue to satisfy their needs?

It's also possible for a Mastermind group not to work out at all and to completely die out after just a few meetings. You can be sure that if participants find that they have not gotten any benefit from it, they will not show up anymore. If the group environment feels too heavy, if participants don't acknowledge each other as peers, if trust does not emerge, if participants do not take the risk of engaging with others, or if the facilitator is not credible or competent, then no framework can be created and built upon.

The facilitator can then recruit other participants to make up for those who have left, or she/he can start a totally new group. Perhaps it is only with more experience, and with other participants, that she/he will find the formula that will bring satisfaction to "her/his" Mastermindians.

When we address the matter of the duration of the existence of a Mastermind group, it brings us to look, again, at the fundamental issue of the inclusion of new members, or that of replacing members who have left the group. Since the group is a living, breathing organism, these changes are only natural and should even be favored at times (these issues are dealt with elsewhere in this book).

To guarantee that your Mastermind group will last over the long haul, you, as facilitator, should make an effort to regularly evaluate participants' satisfaction. There are different ways to accomplish that. We will talk about them again later.

If trust has been established between the Mastermindians in a group, including the facilitator, and a high quality alliance emerges between members, and progress is made by the those members, then that group will last a lot longer.

4.4 How Does the Facilitator Make a Mastermind Group Attractive and Long-Lasting?

The facilitator will, once again, think about how she/he will be able to make her/his Mastermind group last a long time. She/He needs to figure out how to make it more attractive, dynamic, and beneficial for each and every participant. If the group is actually like that, you can be sure that the Mastermindians will do everything to make sure that the group exists all long as possible. Word of mouth will attract new requests from people to join.

The Mastermind group is a place where each participant can get advice, exchange ideas, get certain kinds of services, and go up to a higher level of performance. During the first year, the participants exchange a great many pieces of advice, talk about their personal experiences, offer opinions, and share ideas. They also share their experience of the group, and the emotions they feel while in it, as well as the development techniques they have used. During this initial period, the mutual benefits are very great. All the facilitator has to do is carefully guide the process so that emerging ideas become activated. After this initial period, the duration of which is variable, participants might feel like they have learned everything they possibly can, so the facilitator might feel the need to inject some energy into the group's activity. And there will be a lot of chances for that.

To give an illustration of the kind of tactics that might be used to energize a Mastermind group, the following is a fictionalized overview of what it's like to be on the hot seat (along with the booster process). It starts with a question from a Johnny (Christophe), who is already a facilitator of a Mastermind group, and who is asking for help in another Mastermind group, facilitated by Jeff. The latter, in this instance, is going to be nothing more than just another participant…

Example of the Kind of Work That Takes Place During a Hot Seat Session

The launching of a hot seat session

(Christophe starts recording the session on his cell phone.)

Jeff: *Christophe, because you asked, you can go onto the hot seat and present us with the question you have prepared.*

Christophe: *OK, thanks. I want you to help me today with getting me to the point where I can energize my Mastermind group all over again. It has now been about two years since I first facilitated a group of eight people. We work in an effective manner; we are able to help each other out. We meet every two months on a Saturday. We named the group "Companions for Success". It works really well. I do, however, sense some laxity on the part of some of the participants, since, for the first time, there were three people who were absent from the last meeting. I feel as if these absences are a message that is meant to alert me. So I have a desire to inject new life into the group. I'm asking you to please give me some ideas for strengthening the dynamics of my Mastermind group, so that the participants will be satisfied. I want the Mastermindians to think of our meetings as the most important thing on their schedules.*

The co-mastermindians impressions

Jeff (addressing the other Mastermindians): *OK. Can you tell us what you felt when you listened to Christophe's presentation?*

Cathy: *I felt that you want to offer a very high quality of service to the rest of your Mastermindians. That's great, but it bothers me a little because I have the impression that you're trying to do much more than is necessary.*

Nadia: *You're super-positive as usual, Christophe. I like that.*

Laurent: *I don't find that your question addresses a situation that is all that demanding of you. You know how to energize a group really well, and you ask us this kind of question just the same. I frankly think that you would have been able to ask for our help about some higher-level need.*

Céline: *I feel as if you are kind of uneasy, and I'm wondering if your Mastermind group participants feel the same kind of uncertainty, too, which might explain part of what you feel as disengagement, and which would just be a reflection of your own worries, rather than a lack of interest on their part.*

Éric: *I felt there was a lack of alignment somewhere. I just don't know where.*

Olivier: *I would have liked to have heard more enthusiasm in your presentation. What I heard sounded too factual for me. It lacked vitality… Except that, I, in fact, ask myself the same questions as you, since that resonates well with me.*

Sequence of questions directed at Johnny

Jeff (addressing the Mastermindians): *Thanks. And now I would like everyone to ask Christophe questions so he can clarify things. Christophe, you don't have to give any answers right now. You can do that later if you want.*

Nadia: *Have you spoken to the participants about those absences? Have you asked them the reason for their absences? It's them, your Mastermindians, who are the experts when it comes to this situation.*

Laurent: *What do you want them to say about your Mastermind group?*

Olivier: *Where do you meet? How do you choose the places?*

Cathy: *What kind of facilitator do you want to be? Who is it you want to see when you look at yourself in the mirror?*

Céline: *And if you are mistaken? If it is found that they are all super happy about your organized activities? How are you able to check for that?*

Éric: *Do you put them into the COACH state at the beginning of meetings, as a matter of course?*

Nadia: *How many different processes do you use?*

Céline: *Is the frequency of your meetings the right one?*

Cathy: *What did you do to choose the participants you wanted for your Mastermind group? Did you choose people who are dynamic and ambitious enough?*

Laurent: *How would you know if they are satisfied, and what they would like to experience differently?*

Nadia: *What organized activities do you offer them, between meetings, to maintain creative tension, and to make them think positively about the up-coming meeting? How do you communicate with them to give them the desire to attend, but also to prepare them to be on the hot seat?*

Etc.

Advice and Recommendations

Jeff (to Christophe): *Christophe, can you tell us what you felt when you heard these questions?*

Christophe: *Thanks, everyone. In fact, I've already received a lot of answers to my questions, and I realize, like you said a short while ago, Laurent, that my challenge goes well beyond my question. I realize that part of the answer has to do with my position as facilitator. I've already heard a lot, and already see things a lot differently. Thanks.*

Jeff: *Thanks, Christophe. I would also like to say a word about what I felt since the beginning of the hot seat session. It seems to me that what you are asking is to find out how to make your Mastermind group more desirable, or in other words, how you can make it last longer. Is that right?*

Christophe: *Yes, I think that one might be able to say something like that. So that the group can last. Yes, that's it.*

Jeff (to the other Mastermindians): *OK. All of you can now contribute all the advice that seems pertinent to you in this case.... Advice and ideas...*

Cathy: *Take your participants to fantasy-style places. There are more of them than one might think, and they're often a lot closer than one might think. Let's talk about them afterwards, so I can give you the addresses. That would be really great for all of you.*

Nadia: *I think you should check to see if all of your participants are dynamic enough.*

Laurent: *Stop this group, build it up all over again, and turn it into another.*

Olivier: *Or rather, stop this group but keep its core, which should be made up of the most dynamic of the participants, so you can create another group.*

Nadia: *Or create a second group to go along with the other one.*

Cathy: *Carry out a survey with some of the participants in order to find out what they appreciate, what they would like to change, and what they would like to experience, if they could conjure it up with a magic wand.*

Olivier: *To evaluate their satisfaction with the group, it is necessary for the responses to be anonymous. They will then be more pertinent. You can also target the questions at what they would like to improve.*

Jeff: *Increase the cost of the group so that only the most motivated people remain.*

Olivier: *Organize other kinds of activities for them. Move away from the hot seat. Think about offering other processes.*

Laurent: *Ask experts to come and hold highly specialized talks about subjects that are of interest to the group's members.*

Olivier: *Yeah, have Roger Federer, Jennifer Aniston, Richard Branson, or Bill Clinton come in.*

Cathy: *Or a NYSE manager. I know some of them. I can give you some addresses.*

Olivier: *Hold a meeting in the middle of the White house's garden.*

Nadia: *I have a better idea—in a space shuttle!*

Céline: *Hold a meeting in a really great restaurant. They'll remember that for a very long time.*

Laurent: *I really like the idea of having some experts come in. You need to come up with a list of really great or famous people that you might have show up, and who won't kill you with what they charge.*

Céline: *Change the group's name.*

Nadia: *Recruit some people who seem more motivated, and suggest, to those who seem bored, that they leave the group. You know that it's the quality of the participants which determines the quality of the group. If you have good people, there's no way that there is going to be any kind of laxity.*

Cathy: *Good idea. Try to recruit some top-level people—some business managers, entrepreneurs, inventors.*

Laurent: *Find a way to maintain a high level of energy. Alternate between workshops and periods of relaxation. Carry out workshops on your feet, or in a public park...*

Jeff: *Thanks, everyone. Any final ideas?*

Céline: *Yes, carry out a meeting during a nature hike, or along the path to Compostela, in France and Spain.*

Johnny's Impressions

Jeff (to Christophe): *Christophe, can you give us some feedback about what you felt and got out of this meeting?*

"Give us some feedback and tell us how you feel".

Christophe: *Wow! Was it ever super! Thanks! I am leaving with a thousand ideas, and what's more, some ideas that are going to be easy to implement.*

Concrete Action Plan

Jeff: *Great! And what are the ideas that seem as if they are going to be able to be quickly implemented?*

Christophe (after 5 minutes of reflection): *Well, I will come up with an evaluation questionnaire that I am going to ask participants to fill out. I will also ask if some of them want to take a break from or leave the group. I have had requests from other people who want to join a Mastermind group. Up till now, I felt that it wasn't right to force participants to leave, but I'm now convinced that it can be done, as long as one uses a little bit of tact. I'm also going to change the locations of the meetings and look for places that are even nicer, or which have historical or cultural meaning. For the moment, we are meeting in the backroom of a pretty country hotel that has access to a very beautiful garden that is always in bloom. But I could do better and change locations, in order to create, at every turn, some change in the surroundings. I'm also going to think about having people who are experts on certain subjects come to our group; but for the moment, I don't really know whom.*

Johnny's feelings

Jeff: How do you feel right now?

Christophe: Frankly, I feel lighter. A whole lot lighter. My mind is now filled with a lot of ideas. I am super happy. Thanks a lot.

Commitment and Anchoring of Action

Jeff: Can you make a commitment to do what you have said you will?

Christophe: Yes, of course. It will be easy to do what I have just said I will do. I will do it. I'll give you an update at the next meeting.

Co-Mastermindian Lessons and Impressions

The facilitator asks each participant what the experience of the hot seat session has been like for her/him, and what she/he has learned from it.

End of the hot seat session, using the Booster process.

The fictionalized session described above would actually last between 45 minutes and an hour. It allows us to define (since that was the goal) a certain number of methods that can be used to make a Mastermind group more dynamic, desirable, and sustainable:

* By going to places that hold meaning, are innovative, or exceptionally beautiful, and which are conducive to creativity: historical, cultural, or religious sites, such as museums, rehabilitated industrial buildings, attractive luxury hotels, artists' residences, modern architectural space, design centers, superb-looking clearings, in-bloom public park, old abbeys, etc. It's a long list!

* By having some experts intervene by talking about subjects that interest the Mastermindians.

* By having famous people come in.

* By reinvigorating the participants by bringing in new blood (based on rules that are eventually co-defined with the rest of the participants).

* By asking those who are least active (even procrastinators) to be kind enough to let other participants take over their places.

* By changing the workshops and the facilitation processes.

* By proceeding with surveys to become more familiar with and understand Mastermindian expectations.

* By alternating work activities and recreational workshops.

* By providing great food.

* By improving the quality of the participants' welcome.

That is a really good list of effective solutions, that is to say, of concrete benefits; but at the same time, Johnny has accumulated some other, non-concrete benefits: the lessening of his discomfort, self-confidence, time saving in the future, etc.

In less than an hour. Not so bad... Right?

4.5 How Many Participants?

We, the authors, have shared a great many discussions on this issue. There are no rules as far as the number of participants is concerned, but there are certain principles that should be adhered to.

We believe that the Mastermind group dynamic can be triggered off, even if it is launched with just two people. Two-person groups are referred to as "two partners who share in responsibility". This duo does not, of course, benefit from the dynamics of a larger group, but it's a good start. The pair will then be able to recruit other participants so that the group becomes more powerful and becomes a true Mastermind group. The full power of the group dynamics, in all probability, will only manifest itself when there are at least four or five participants. In spite of a commitment to attend every meeting, there are often some absent people. Because of this, a group that is supposed to have five people will often meet with just four. In that case, the facilitator can also act as a participant so that the exchanges will be richer. Obviously, the more restricted the number of those in the group, the more important is their the commitment to attend.

We know some consultants who manage (with assistants) Mastermind groups made up of 40 participants. Others have even more participants, sometimes hundreds of them! But we think, at that point, that it is no longer a Mastermind group but more like a seminar. We feel that the Mastermind group should remain one whose numbers are restricted. A Mastermind group is not some kind of factory. The generally accepted limit, when one is talking about a restricted attendance group, is no more that 15 people. If there are more participants than that, it is no longer a restricted group, and its dynamics will work differently. If there are more than a dozen participants, it will be difficult for the facilitator to continue to come up with things which are of a high quality work (like haute couture!) and to concern herself/himself with every one of the Mastermindians. If there are more than a dozen participants, there's a possibility that there will be too many interactions between them. It then becomes difficult to get to know each one of them; that can have a negative impact on the creation of trust.

We think that the maximum number of participants that a facilitator should manage is 10. This number allows one to carry out the processes we have described rather easily, and everyone has a chance to express herself/himself. It also allows the creation of closeness between the Mastermindians, which is necessary for the emergence of trust, and which is very important when it comes to the pertinence of exchanges and the richness of what is to be shared. If there are more than 10 people, certain participants will not be able to talk. That will create dissatisfaction, which is something that will quickly damage the group. If there are more than 10 participants, the facilitator will want to have a two-person team or assistant who is also well-versed in the art of collective support.

10 participants is the maximum but not ideal number. Have you already tried to coordinate the schedules of 10 people to come up with a date for a meeting that lasts an entire day? It seems to us that a group of 7 people is the best option at any level. The ideal number, according to Jack Canfield, author of *The Success Principles*[1], is six.

The ideal number of participants will depend, of course, on the type of processes that the facilitator has decided to lead, and on her/his experience in the area of collective support (and on the Mastermindians' capacity for disciplined behavior during meetings). A facilitator who regularly carries out sessions that are purely instructive can manage more participants than an other facilitator who leads processes that support the emergence of collective intelligence, which is based on trust.

The facilitator who wants to do Mastermind groups with a lot of participants will therefore carry out more sessions that are purely instructive and will lead efforts that are more typical, such as brainstorming work in sub-groups, the results of which are then shared in a special session, with comments by the facilitator (who is, at that time, wearing his trainer's hat). One might think that large groups would offer more resources, more experience, and more ideas; but the challenges of large group dynamics can make it difficult to allow those things to emerge and be shared as effectively as in a restricted group.

---

4   Canfield, J., *The Success Principles: How to Get from Where You are to Where You Want to Be,* 2005, Harper Collins Publishers.

The frequency and length of meetings can have an influence on the maximum number of participants. A group that meets often (once a week), or over a long period of time (several days), will be able to take in more members than one that rarely meets, or for short periods of time. What is essential is that each Mastermindian fully benefit from her/his participation and be satisfied by what she/he has gotten out of it in terms of ideas, advice, decisions, and her/his progress as a human being. To achieve that, we think that it is necessary for each person to go onto the hot seat a minimum of once every two months.

4.6 Frequency, Duration, and Pace of Meetings

The Mastermind group's organizer will choose its temporal structure. She/He will eventually make it evolve, depending on participants' requests and preferences, and the issues they bring to the group. It seems necessary to us that Mastermindians periodically be able to see one another in person. That should take place, at a minimum, every three months, in order to maintain the quality and intensity of the generative field, although we will see later that some groups meet only once a year. In the third part of this book, an example of its structure is presented: a one-year commitment, three in-person meetings, lasting two days, and 3 webinars (video conferences). It is just one example among many others. Each facilitator will make her/his own choices.

The frequency and length of meetings are closely related factors. If the group meets often (at least once a month), a half-day session is, for the most part, sufficient. On the other hand, if it meets only rarely (twice a year), she/he will be interested in planning an in-person meeting that will last two or three days. Likewise, if the number of participants is greater than 12, some meetings that last at least two days will be needed so that each person benefits from going onto the hot seat.

Participation Ratio

To find out if a group is the right size and meets the right number of times, the facilitator should calculate her/his group's participation ratio. That allows her/him to know if the group offers participants enough opportunities to go onto the hot seat. To find that out, all she/he has to do is calculate the number of opportunities that a single participant will have on the hot seat during a year. For example, a group that meets 10 times a year, and which offers three hot seat sessions a day has, at its disposal, enough time to offer up to 30 such sessions per year. This number should be divided by the number of participants to get the number of possible hot seat sessions. 30 such sessions, when there are 20 participants, corresponds to a ratio of 1.5 sessions per year, per person. That isn't very much. The higher the ratio, the more opportunity there is for the participants to benefit from the use of the hot seat.

So she/he can determine the best frequency for holding sessions, the facilitator will put herself/himself in the place of the participants, depending on their profiles, or the kind of profiles that reflect that kind of people she/he is seeking for her/his group. If the planned frequency corresponds with their availability and the commitment they are capable of making, then the group will run smoothly. For example, some business leaders might not be able to commit to one day per month but might be free for a half-day each month. In the case of an existing Mastermind group, the facilitator, if she/he feels it is necessary, will have the group reflect on this matter and decide along with her/him. The facilitator will find out that the frequency and length of her/his Mastermind group's meetings will depend a lot on the participants' profiles and availability. She/He should adapt the group structure accordingly.

Participants' Taking of Action

The participants' taking of action is another element that should be taken into consideration. If a group only meets once a month, it will be difficult for participants to take action and then evaluate the effects of that action. The facilitator will need to take this into account so she/he can come up with a good rhythm or pace for her/his group.

Weekly Meetings

When meetings are held weekly, things move forward quickly and everyone has the chance to go onto the hot seat several times, and within a shorter frame of time. It is a very rapid pace that reflects the extreme motivation of professionals who have started some activity and have need of multiple ideas, advice, and encouragement, and who are ready to run with all of that for a while. It is, on the other hand, a pace that can be rather burdensome. People have a hard time being available to participate on a weekly basis, so there is a risk that one's motivation will decrease. Be careful not to overdo it. The length of each weekly meeting runs anywhere from two to four hours. A meal can be shared at the end of that type of meeting.

Some groups meet every 15 days. That is a pace that, because of its regularity, might be good for a group that is just forming.

There is a Mastermind model known as "Sprint," in which people meet every week, for two or three months, so that strong dynamics are created in the core group. The number of meetings are later reduced, to one per month, for example. This rather nerve-racking format is reserved for very motivated participants who want to progress quickly.

Monthly Meetings

Monthly or bi-monthly meetings seem to us to be a good rhythm for participants. The Mastermindians have more time during which they can prepare to go onto the hot seat, and above all, to turn their commitments into action.

The length of a monthly meeting could be a half or whole day. The latter scenario increases, for each Mastermindian, the number of opportunities to go onto the hot seat. One can plan to have 3 to 5 Johnny's on the hot seat in a single day, and the facilitator will have more time for complementary contributions, or for allowing an expert to intervene.

Quarterly Meetings

Some Mastermind groups only meet two to four times a year. There is no risk of overdoing it. These are, generally speaking, Mastermind groups made up of entrepreneurs and high-level business leaders who have a hard time finding free time for the group in their schedules. They meet then for two or three days, under seminar-like circumstances, in places that are, generally speaking, quite pleasant. So the whole experience has a vacation-like feel about it.

Because these meetings are so rare, the Mastermindians expect to get a whole lot from them. It is interesting to see how collective negotiations take place so that the date for the next meeting can be determined. To avoid any scheduling problems, it is better to roughly stick to the same dates for each year, for example, "every year, during the last weekend of January, and the first weekend in July".

Yearly Meetings

A once-a-year meeting is set aside for participants whose schedules are super busy, and who, because of that, find that they have a hard time being available. They know, in advance, that they will meet every year, often as part of a fringe activity at large national gatherings, or national or international congresses for entrepreneurs, like the Davos Economic Forum in Switzerland. Admission to this kind of Mastermind group is generally carried out through cooptation between high-level people, or through people who acknowledge one another as such.

Scheduling of Sessions

It matters little if the meetings take place in the morning, afternoon, or evening. One might, of course, say that people think more clearly during the morning than in the afternoon, and even much more so than in the evening. But each facilitator and group will decide what seems the best.

It is only in the case of remote international Mastermind groups (video conference), which bring together participants from all over the world, that the exact schedule for meetings is extremely important. If a group accepts people from the Americans, Europe and Asia it will, of course, be necessary to fine tune schedules so that the meetings can take place. When certain participants will be attending in the morning, and others in the evening, for example, it will be difficult to hold meetings that last more than a few hours at a time.

4.7 Seminars that Last Several Days

When seminars roll out over a period of several days, it is appropriate, even necessary, for meetings to be relocated to a site far removed from daily life, such as a vacation-style place site, or one that is, at the least, very beautiful. We have already pointed out how the quality of a venue has an influence on the quality of discussions, which are good for freeing up emotional reactions, and for the quality of memories of the event that each participant will preserve inside of her/his mind for a long time.

Seminars that take place over several days can be coordinated with one's regular vacation. For example, a Mastermind group that is going to meet for three days in Miami (or Hawaii, the French Riviera or Tokyo) can be planned at the same time at, and the same place, that one decides to take a family vacation. Nevertheless, evenings with the family will only be possible if the facilitator has not scheduled evening sessions, of course. Would you find that having morning, mid-day, and evening sessions would be too much? It's just that you, in all likelihood, have not yet experienced the feeling of happiness that comes from participating in a group whose members have a symbiotic relationship with one another. We want you to experience that one day. It becomes such a wonderful experience that time doesn't matter anymore. The intimate nature of sessions that last several days generate even more moments of pleasure, co-responsibility, and alignment. As far as seminars that last over several days are concerned, we strongly advise that several kinds of procedures be used: hot seats, brainstorming, co-coaching, going for walks with two or three other groups members and exchanging ideas, instructional sessions, interventions by well-known personalities, etc.

And of course, the seminars are a chance for Mastermindians to enjoy meals, or Spanish inn-style sandwiches, with other participants. For Mastermindians who only meet rarely, the sessions have a sacred quality, and they cannot imagine missing any of them, because of the pleasure that comes about from the meetings themselves, seeing the other Mastermindians again, knowing that they are going to leave with a lot of really great ideas, spending really good moments with her/his fellow Mastermindians, and that which comes from helping one another out and moving forward with things together... We guarantee that, at the end of just one session, all Mastermindians will turn into friends and feel like family.

The group dynamic that is created during the Mastermind sessions is very valuable. Physical proximity brings about psychological closeness, trust, and the deepest kind of bonds, which will feed discussions and result in all kinds of benefits in the future. The facilitator can rent a lodge that will be large enough to accommodate everyone, and which will have an activities room, or will ensure that every participant has a room reserved at the same hotel.

We also advise groups that meet for a half-day, or one day per month, to plan a yearly seminar that will take place over several days.

Let's sum everything up below. Each one of the frequencies, for the sessions, has its advantages and disadvantages:

Frequency	Possible Duration	Advantages	Disadvantages
Weekly	Between 2 and 4 hours.	Each participant gathers a large number of ideas and recommendations, all at once. The development of possible projects speeds up quite a bit.	Risk that the participants will become tired. The fact that any specific group might only be a possibility for those who live in close proximity to one another.
Monthly to tri-monthly	A half- or complete day.	A laid back pace for participants who are sufficiently motivated because of the success they are having.	A priori, none.
Two or three meetings per year	One to two days.	It allows one to have one or two evenings to spend more time together. A possibility of moving meetings to exotic places. It allows for closeness to be created between participants.	Rather limited frequency. Bonds run the risk of breaking down somewhat between meetings. There is a need to host face-to-face video conferences so that the relational field can be maintained, and so there can be verification that participants have taken action. Proximity can create discomfort. It can make or break the situation (it, generally speaking, makes it).

Frequency	Possible Duration	Advantages	Disadvantages
Yearly	One to three days.	This format allows business leaders and entrepreneurs who are very busy to see one another once a year, so they can take stock of things and work quickly on very hot topics related to them or their businesses. These meetings generally take place on the fringes of some big business event (a forum, symposium, general meeting, etc.).	The low frequency of meetings hardly allows for the creation of trust and bonds. This type of format targets high-level entrepreneurs and top business leaders who acknowledge one another as such.

4.8 And Between Meetings?

The facilitator might still be very active between meetings, but group members can also do a lot of things on their own. They might call one another or decide to meet so they can help each other out, create something, or do some business together. They might challenge one another. They might see one another to socialize, spend some relaxing time together, do some sport, or go to a restaurant. They might participate in other activities and trainings together. Who knows just what they might do? And they don't need a facilitator for any of that. It is good, for the dynamics of the group, for there to be a lot of interaction between the Mastermindians. This is proof of the group's strength, and of its added value for each Mastermindian.

For groups that meet often, that is to say, at least once a month, the facilitator should ensure "a minimum amount of organized activity" by responding to members' questions, and by sending out invitations to future meetings. But for Masterminds who meet less frequently, the facilitator will assume an important role in making sure that relational bonds stay strong, and by checking on the progress of group members. She/He might decide to set up some online meetings, for example, at least one a month, to maintain the group bond and its dynamics. It is completely possible to carry out hot seat sessions during a video conference, and even over the phone! There is less of a feeling of pleasure, in that case, of course, than when it takes place in person; but its effectiveness is potentially the same.

Here is a short list of organized activities that the facilitator might implement between meetings:

* She/He might host video conference Mastermind meetings.

* She/He might call participants to ask them if they are carrying out the actions that they said they would, and if they are working on their project, in general.

* She/He might contribute technical (instructional) elements that have seemed necessary to her/him at the time of face-to-face meetings.

* She/He can keep an eye out for relevant documentation, and send documents and links to the participants, or offer other reading material that is related to their projects.

* She/he can kindly challenge participants and incite them to stick to their commitments and accomplish their goals.

* She/he can ask participants if they need advice or help and ask other Mastermindians to throw their support behind them.

* Or undertake any other initiative that seems pertinent to her/him!

The pains that the facilitator takes to moves thing forward during the time between sessions will have a strong influence on the carrying out of commitments on the part of the Mastermindians; also on their motivation, and on the memories that are being created as a result of the group's venture.

A Shared Space on the Web

Since a Mastermind group is essentially based on collaborative dynamics, it is appropriate to use every kind of collaborative resource, including communication technologies. We have already looked at webinars, but there are a lot of other collaborative resources on the Internet that are often free. You should, however, be careful about confidentiality when it comes to adding anything on collaborative platforms. Obviously, you shouldn't put anything on them that should remain secret. Most "modern" work groups use tools that are shared on the Web, which address issues associated with online work, asynchronous work, and capitalizing on work that is carried out. As long as one uses the precautions we have mentioned, these collaborative tools definitely have a place when it comes to the functioning of a Mastermind group. Let's mention, from among numerous tools, just a few:

* Shared or collaborative boards (for example, Yahoo groups, Google groups, Slack)

* Shared schedules (Google agenda)

* Tools for choosing dates, and for surveys (for example, Doodle)

* Word processing programs and shared spreadsheets (for example, Loomio, Google Docs)

* Shared task management (for example, Asana and Trello)

* Files storage (for example, Dropbox)

Other than their obvious usefulness when it comes to sharing things, these tools strengthen the feeling of belonging in group members.

4.9 Online Meetings (Webinars and Video Conferences)

A webinar or video conference is a meeting that takes place on the Internet. It allows all kinds of teams to meet online and work together, no matter at what location they happen to be. Many free Internet platforms offer video conference services that work well for up to 10 or 12 participants. However, free platforms offer no guarantee of confidentiality; so if you discuss things on them that are of a highly sensitive nature, it will, in all likelihood, be necessary for you to make use of secure video conference services, for which you will have to pay. Platforms that have to be paid for offer several interesting technical options: they welcome a great many participants, active management, the sharing of screens, access through phone calls or through a video conference, surveys, the sharing of documents, recordings of discussions, and more.

The facilitator sees to it that discussions do not veer off into an exchange of banal comments. If she/he feels that it is necessary, she/he will regulate the quality of exchanges and will allot speaking time. As you will see, participation in a video conference requires some discipline, in particular when it comes to the management of the activation/deactivation of microphones; if not managed properly, the exchanges quickly become inaudible, and the feedback will make the meeting impossible. If a request for a session on the hot seat comes up, the facilitator and members of the group will decide together what follow-up should be given to it, that is to say, if it is OK now or at a time in the near future. If a Mastermindian requests a booster seat session, and the request is OK'd, then obviously, the session takes place.

Hosting and participating in a webinar requires a special kind of discipline. The effectiveness of this tool will be compromised if the rigor of the host is not at the right level. Therefore, the host will take all the time that she/he needs to train herself/himself on how to use all the functionalities of the online platform. She/He will also set aside the time that is needed for helping participants become quickly connected if they are not familiar with the video conference tool that is being used. Attention should be paid to this last point, because if there are connection problems, an online meeting can be ruined. That would make the host look like a real amateur.

A hot seat session can be conducted online in almost the same way that it is in person. Online meetings, however, can be affected by sequences of information about each individual participant's progress. It can be formatted as follows:

* My emotional state today

* Here is what I want from our online meeting today (goal).

* Here is what happened for me since the last time we saw one another, and what I did (feedback).

* Here is what I am bringing up because of difficult situations (explanation of progress that is yet to be accomplished).

* And here is what I would like to gather some opinions and advice about, from the rest of my co-Mastermindians (beginning of an online hot seat session).

The length of a participant's webinar hot seat session might be limited to about 20 minutes. That is enough time for each Mastermindian to make some very valuable contributions. These focused contributions, which might only last about 20 minutes per Mastermindian (no matter what procedure is used), allow the webinar to take place inside of a 2 or 3 hour time frame. Some meetings can be longer, but the participants' concentration will suffer, as a result.

It is useful to remember that, during a webinar, the participants are not at the same level of attention that they are when they are at an in-person meeting. They might look at their e-mails, at the same time that they are attending the webinar, or they might get disrupted because of things that are going on at that same time, either professionally, or with their family, in the background. The host should ensure that the level of online activity remains very intense so that the participants are much more likely to pay close attention to what is going on. In that case, the work that will be carried out should turn out to be effective.

4.10 Mastermind Groups that Are Only (or Almost Only) Online

Some facilitators only offer Mastermind groups online. This, obviously, is not the best format; we think that in-person groups are more effective, but the former still works, just the same. All of the advice given in this book is also valid for Mastermind groups that are only online.

The advantages of this format are:

* The costs for organized activities are lower since no logistics are involved: No meeting room has to be located, no traveling expenses are incurred, and no food or beverages have to be brought in from anywhere.

* It saves time for participants since they don't have to travel to a physical location.

* The Mastermind group becomes something that is more affordable since it can be launched at a reasonable cost (the cost of a Mastermind group that is only online should not be all that high).

But Mastermind groups are only totally held online rarely. We think that the facilitator should plan for an in-person two- or three-day gathering of Mastermindians. Participants will be very willing to come so they can meet their "peers in progress"; they will definitely take a great deal of pleasure in having face-to-face interactions with them. It will be an experience that will be all the more powerful for them when participants show up from many different parts of the world.

4.11 The Cost of a Mastermind Group

Before talking in any great detail about the issue of cost, one has to wonder, in the first place, whether it's really necessary for a Mastermind group to have a participation fee. The answer to this question is no. The Mastermind group that the eight authors of this book are members of does not charge one. And for very good reason—we function according to the principles of collective intelligence. We don't have any "official" facilitator; we are, instead, just the group's eight regular facilitators.

As has already been expressed, any individual can decide to create "her/his" own Mastermind group, as soon as she/he has some knowledge about them. And she/he doesn't have to force participants to pay a fee. The person who has initiated the group is paid then in the form of advice and support that she/he will receive from others. Some Mastermind groups are made up of people who are looking for work; each person helps the others to find a job (at the highest level possible, of course).

However, we do believe that if participants pay to be a part of a Mastermind group, they will be highly motivated to achieve their goals. In every kind of work where there is a psychological component involved, paying for participation is something that is to be preferred, even if the payment is a modest amount. Of what value is free advice? If an expert gives you some advice after you run across her/him on a street corner, or if you pay for the same advice, would the first scenario, in your eyes, be of more value? We can almost bet that that wouldn't be the case. Some facilitators might offer participants a group for which they have to pay at least something, based on their conscience; that is a system whereby each individual pays what she/he deems to be the right amount. The financial gains that might come about, in that instance, are always uncertain and variable.

You should still think of the Mastermind group is an investment; and since it is, there should be no problem when it comes to asking for a fee for it. When the facilitator states that a Mastermind group is an investment, she/he is guaranteeing participants that the gains and advantages they are going to reap from their participation will greatly exceed the amount of money and time they are going to invest in it. Whatever its cost, the Mastermind group should therefore be profitable; if it isn't, there is no reason for it to exist. If you participate in a Mastermind and end up feeling that you are not going to profit from your investment, you might as well quit it and look for another one later on.

The cost of a Mastermind group amounts to a flat entrance fee. One does not pay for one meeting at a time; it is always a long-term commitment that, generally speaking, rolls out over a defined span of time. The facilitator can decide to authorize one or several trial sessions so that it can be determined if the candidate has the right kind of desire to participate and compatibility with the rest of the group. After that, the length of her/his participation is, generally speaking, one year.

The cost of participation depends on several different parameters: how many meetings are held every year, where these meetings take place, the facilitator's rating, the Mastermindians social level, what the successes, thanks to this Mastermind group, have been, what the current Mastermindians say, etc.

The costs can sometimes be surprising. If a well-known consultant is able to recruit some people of rather substantial means into her/his group, she/he might charge some very high fees.

Here is what we know and feel about fees that were being applied at the time we wrote this book:

* There are some virtual Mastermind groups, that is to say, those that are only carried out through video conferencing, whose fee amounts to a few hundred dollars per year.

* A yearly fee of $5,000 to $10,000, excluding tax, to attend a Mastermind group that meets once a month, seems reasonable to us.

* We know of a European Mastermind group that meets four times a year, for three days at a time, in really beautiful (so it costs more). It charges 12,000 euro, excluding tax.

* We know of a Mastermind group that charges $25,000 for three-day gatherings which take place three times a year.

* There are, in all likelihood, Mastermind groups that are even more expensive than that. Those would be put on for Stock Exchange or Wall Street managers.

* If the Mastermind group meets in person, there are often costs related to logistics that are added on to the cost of organized activities: traveling, lodging, and food and beverages.

* When meetings take place in luxury locations, or at different places throughout the world, additional costs related to travel and lodging can be very high.

The cost that the facilitator decides on is also a way for her/him to be selective about the kind of participants she/he recruits. Facilitators are able to determine the fee for their Mastermind groups as a function of the clientele on whom they believe they will be able to have an effect. It is better if there is not too much difference in social status between Mastermindians. The fee ensures that there will be consistency among the kind of participants who are chosen.

It is, however, possible to accept a participant who is of a lower social class than the others. The ability of such a member to generate a significant amount of money so that she/he can join a Mastermind group, even when she/he has been of limited means, is an indication that she/he is determined to succeed. That kind of member is probably a good acquisition for the group, because she/he will be very motivated and will bring a positive kind of dynamic into it.

To reassure some people who are afraid that they will not have enough money to participate, the facilitator might, in at least a couple of cases, allow them to do so free of charge, "to see how things turn out", or guarantee a total reimbursement if, after two or three trial days, the person decides that she/he does not want to continue.

We hope that every facilitator will remember that a Mastermind group is not something that should be construed as a money maker, or as a cash cow, but as a builder of relationships and a high quality service for a group of people who want to progress, socially and professionally, in the areas of business and leadership, and to succeed together. For the facilitator, above all if she/he puts the principles of collective intelligence in place, the pay off should be thought of as an outcome and not as a goal. Remember the following principle: One should, first of all, give to others, or Give first!

Drawing on all of the information we have already shared about the concept known as the Mastermind group, we offer a formalized description (or presentation brief) of one below:

Mastermind Group's Name: Explorers of the Emerging Future

Group's Condition (existing group or in the process of being created): In the Process of Creation

Targeted Population: Entrepreneurs

More Specifically: Leaders of companies that have been in existence for more than 2 years, and which have generated sales of more than $300,000, and who want to unleash their company's potential.

Group Size:

Minimum Number of Participants: 5

Maximum Number of Participants: 10

Language Held In: English

Group's Purpose:

The purpose of this group is to sustain the development of Mastermindians' business endeavors, by surrounding them with a high level of attention, directed at their specific issues. These managers formulate their vision, mission, and ambition in relation to their business endeavors. They discover solutions and share them amongst themselves.

Frequency and Pace of Meetings:

Type of Meetings:

Number of In-Person Meetings: 7 day-long meetings, and a 2-day seminar

Number of Online Meetings: 7

Length of Commitment: A minimum of one year, renewable at the end of each year.

Candidate Recruiting Methods:

Initial Steps for Candidate: Must give answers to a questionnaire, during a video conference or face-to-face interview, verification of goals while in the group, and that she/he has the right kind of ambition.

Steps Required for Joining the Group: All of the above, and then a meeting during which a trial is carried out, and then validation by the Mastermindians, based on a "no strong objections" method (the candidate is rejected if there is one or more strong objections to her/his joining).

Cost: $10,000 per year, which includes food and beverages (but not transportation or lodging).

Chapter 5

How to Recruit Participants for Your Mastermind Group

5.1 Who Can Join a Mastermind Group?

We think that every individual who feels that she/he is "an entrepreneur at heart" should be allowed to join a Mastermind group. To be a Mastermindian, a person needs to want to be more than what she/he currently is, and to accomplish things that would be difficult to accomplish on her/his own. She/He needs to have a sufficient amount of ambition which, preferably, will be as generous for herself/himself as it will be for the rest of the participants.

Being an entrepreneur at heart means that one has a capacity or desire to develop and create new products or services, and to contribute a wealth of ideas and/or added value. This can correspond with many different professions. People can be self-promoters, starting as CEO's of multinational corporations, but can also be in higher levels of organization, inasmuch as they have the ability to act without having to ask for authorization, or social or union leaders, or politicians. And let's not forget all those who are involved in the creative arts (painters, film makers, actors, singers, musicians, writers, choreographers, etc.) who, quite often, assume an entrepreneurial attitude when it comes to promoting their art, and who are able to contribute a lot of resources to the group in terms of creativity, sensitivity, and opening up to the world. In brief, all those who want to give themselves the means to achieve and even exceed their goals more quickly are more than welcome. All those who want to better succeed, and more quickly at that, inside of an organized, creative, caring, and supportive environment...

Let's imagine that you want to join a Mastermind group. The following are the 10 points or principles that will allow you to see if you would turn out to be a good Mastermindian. You can also answer the questionnaire that's found at the end of this book.

Before you start, it is also a good idea to verify that the group's format and way of functioning is agreeable to you so that you won't waste your time nor the time of the others in the group. We should remind you, that while a member in the group, you are supposed to think about the other members before yourself.

1 – You Need to Be Authentic

The ideal Mastermindian:

* Is authentic: Intellectual honesty is important to her/him. She/he expresses things just as she/he sees them, just the way she/he thinks they are. She/He is honest and caring. She/he pays attention to how she/he feels and does not keep, just for herself/himself, what might be of help for others, even if that's not always easy, and even if it would be easier for her/him to just talk about what is going well.

An ideal Mastermindian knows how he/she feels and behaves congruently..

* Is consistent: This is another form of intellectual integrity. She/He does not act in a duplicitous manner and allows others to interpret her/his attitudes and actions. She/He is the personification of her/his thoughts and values.

* Is factual : She/He rejects illusions and falsehoods. She/He confronts reality just as it is, and not like she/he would like it to be. She/He supports her/his points of view, using concrete facts.

* Knows how to distance herself/himself: She/He knows how to look at things in an objective manner and avoids drama. She/he is able to think about herself/himself as a subject that can be observed and criticized, after which she/he can reconsider her/his beliefs, feelings, values, successes and failures, and her/his criteria for making judgments...

2 – You Need to Be Discreet

The ideal Mastermindian:

* Needs, fundamentally speaking, to be a discreet person. What is said inside of the group needs to remain inside of it. She/He is aware that some of the things that come out of the group's interaction, if expressed elsewhere, outside of their context, could damage other participants and the group's continued existence. But if a project is of real interest, she/he can ask the Mastermindians in question if it is OK if she/he talks about it with other people.

3 – You Need to Know How to Give and Receive

The ideal Mastermindian:

* Understands that she/he is coming to give as much as she/he is going to receive. She/He also knows that from this circle of giving, which is based on the virtuousness of the gift given, she/he will receive, sooner or later, all the wonderful benefits that come about from her/his participation in the group. She/He understands that she/he is enriched, all the more, by adopting the motto of "others first".

* Is generous/liberal-minded: She/he is certain that generosity is a fundamental, necessary value in her/his group of peers. She/He has understood the importance of win-win relationships and does not seek to get as much as she/he can for herself/himself if she/he has not contributed to the success of other members (who are, moreover, complete strangers at the beginning of their relationship).

4 – You Should Be Respectful and Caring

The ideal Mastermindian:

* Is respectful: She/he is sensitive to differences between people, situations, and organizations. She/He is capable of learning, on the basis of comparisons, and her/his differences in relation to others.

* Uses language in a clear, concise way: She/He expresses difficult concepts in a way that is constructive for and acceptable to the person who is listening to her/him.

* Is in the present moment: She/He is fully present in relation to what is being said and taking place. She/He knows how to listen carefully to others at the same time that she/he is tuned in to her/his emotions.

* Does not force her/his own ideas on others because she/he knows that they are not always applicable to others' realities. What she/he thinks is (probably) good for herself/himself but not necessarily for the rest. Because of that, she/he offers her/his ideas and advice, among other things, with self-restraint.

5 – You Should Turn Your Weaknesses into Strengths

The ideal Mastermindian:

* Accepts vulnerability when in this Mastermind group. She/He deposits the armor which she/he is perhaps accustomed to carry elsewhere, in places of power. She/He knows that it serves no purpose with her/his peers. On the contrary, It slows it down and prevents it from advancing. She/He understands that she/he can learn to show her/his vulnerability, and that it will never be used against her/him.

* Shares her/his experiences, so that they will be useful, not only for her/him, but for other Mastermindians, too. She/He calmly talks about her/his failures; everyone learns from that. She/He also talks about her/his successes, in a measured kind of way, so that the others can become aware of the methods that she/he has used.

* Knows how to call things into question: She/He has the great ability to tell herself/himself that she/he is not always right. She/He thinks of herself/himself as a "subject" who can be improved by working on her/his human qualities. Similarly, she/he thinks of her/his ideas as merely proposals that may or may not be pertinent.

* Is humble: She/He is able to control her/his self-defense reflexes (Reactivity during the CRASH state) when her/his peers confront her/him about decisions she/he has made, or about her/his projects, with unpleasant feedback, or when they throw her/his abilities into doubt. She/He doesn't feel rejected even if her//his peers shake her/him up, even if they drive her/him into a corner.

* Wants to progress as a human being: She/He works in areas where she/he should improve: like anger, egotism, fears, etc., so she/he can understand and /respond to them better, and live in harmony with them. She/He is aware that she/he has some unconscious gray areas that sometimes compel her/him to hold beliefs and carry out behaviors that are not necessarily all that noble.

6 – You Should Come to Learn

The ideal Mastermindian:

* Is aware that she/he doesn't know everything: She/He moves along the path of progress with humility.

* Is aware that she/he learns more quickly, and that new things appear because of contact with others. She/He respects her/his peers for everything they have taught her/him.

* Is an avid learner: She/He likes to place herself/himself in the position of learner and remain alert so she/he can learn and make progress along the path of personal and professional development.

* Has the ability to shift focus: She/He knows how to adapt as a function of situations that point to different points of view.

* Is an active learner: She/he knows how to recognize what she/he has learned and to increase its value, and her/his skills and competencies. And she/he likes that.

7 – You Should Be Aware of Things

The ideal Mastermindian:

* Is aware of things: She/He enjoys talking about what she/he is a part of, what goes well about it, as well as what poses difficulties. She/He is able to ask for help when she/he needs it. She/He also knows how to ask questions so that discussions can be opened up. The Mastermindians share, at every meeting, what they have done, the results that were obtained, and what she/he has learned.

8 – You Should Be Ambitious and Enterprising

The ideal Mastermindian:

* Is ambitious: She/He knows what she/he wants, and comes up with a way to act that will lead to her/his success.

* Knows how to define her/his goals: She/He does not move forward randomly. She/He creates plans of action using proven methods, so she/he can achieve clear, concrete, measurable goals.

* Is daring: She/He is always ready to take risks. Once those risks are measured, she/he assumes a daring attitude, moves forward at a rapid pace, and acts on things. And no matter what the result, she/he assumes the consequences for it without condemning anyone else.

* Makes a commitment: She/He makes a commitment to achieve ambitious goals.

* Is transformative, not a dreamer.

* Feels powerful: She/He feels connected to her/his goals, which are powerful. She/He is flooded with them.

9 – You Should Be Trusting

The ideal Mastermindian:

* Is able to trust: She/He offers her/his trust, in the first place, to the members of the group.

* She/He does not struggle with anyone. She/He remains calm and serene; that frees all of her/his energy so she/he can make progress in her/his business, leadership role, and projects, and as a human being.

* Allows herself/himself to be guided: She/He doesn't place the processes that have been proposed to her/him, by the facilitator, in doubt, and does not balk at anything, or moan and groan. She/He trusts the facilitator since she/he is convinced that she/he knows what she/he is doing.

* Is trusting: She/He has an unconditional trust in the future. She/He knows that she/he will always have the resources she/he needs to come out of any situation successfully. And she/he has no fear about anybody stealing her/his ideas. She/He knows that it is because of others that her/his ideas will take on power, to whatever degree they do.

10 – You Should Be Truly Capable of Making Commitments

The ideal Mastermindian: Each member makes a solid, long lasting commitment.

* Every time that a member participates in a session, she/he helps develop the group's capacity for expression, at the same time that a bond of trust is created. If there is not a strong commitment on the part of every member, to participate in Mastermind exchanges, the group will never completely develop.

* Before allowing each accepted candidate into the group, time should be taken to explain to her/him just how crucial and important her/his commitment is going to be for everyone, including herself/himself Provide the schedule for sessions in advance. Ask members to add the sessions to their calendars.

* If a person is unable to participate on a majority of the dates, that means that she/he is not a good candidate for the group.

* Each member shares responsibility in relation to every other member of the group: She/He does not take her/his participation lightly. She/He is very committed to everyone's success. She/He is also committed to the success of the group's collective processes, right along with the facilitator.

* The Mastermindian is constantly present in the "Here and Now" : She/He is diligent and sees to it that the quality of her/his presence is high. Being truly present does not just mean that your body and brain are there—it means that your entire being is present: your mind, emotions, intentions, and motivation. All of that is connected and is supportive of your contribution.

* A high level of commitment, on the part of each member, allows for Mastermind group on which the participants can rely.

5.2 The Mastermind Group

How to create the Group ?

We have already seen that the facilitator is in charge of forming the Mastermind group in the most coherent way possible. It is her/his responsibility to have compatible personalities and complementary skills in the group. The paradox is that the wider the range of competencies, the more rich the exchanges and suggestions will be. It is up to the facilitator to mix the differences with homogeneity. He will also pay attention to the fact that differences in the level of social success are not too great. While novice entrepreneur may find a lot of value in participating in a group of highly successful entrepreneurs, the reverse is unlikely to be the case. A balance must be struck between common points that facilitate mutual understanding, and differences to stimulate discussion.

5.3 Where Does One Find People Who Want to Participate in a Mastermind Group?

Choose people who are already in your professional circle. Go to those who are already in your network: your personal and professional connections – for example, *ANDRH* (human resources association), Medef, Germe, or Apm for individual business directors, groups of business directors, or even the *Facebook* and *LinkedIn* communities or other professional forums.

Look for people who are liberal-minded and have values that reflect a collective frame of mind. Ask them if they know others who would like to join the group…

Create a Meetup group. Meetup brings people who live in thousands of cities together so that they can do what they love together. It's a simple idea: We do what is important to us best when we do it with several others. That's what Meetup does; it brings people together so they can explore ideas, learn, and then take action.

Come up with an event so that your Mastermind group can be discovered by others. Even if the event is free, you can ask participants to show up with a book they can exchange, a good practice they can share, or a donation for a charitable organization. Then, when a small group is created, you can ask each person to invite someone from her/his network, selected on the basis of criteria that is important to the group, so that the circle can be enlarged (sports-oriented, recreational, and professional networks, trade association members, members of miscellaneous clubs).

A personal recommendation offers a powerful kind of leverage. People will, in general, agree to do that spontaneously. Asking for one will allow you to achieve your goals more quickly.

For that, you can also offer an incentive (financial: reduced fee, and/or a bit of your time, a face-to-face coaching session, for example).

You can also invite influential people who will contribute real added value to the group (expert, specialist, motivational speaker).

You can also find some people/groups with which to create some synergies, like, for example, circles made up of business creators or "turn around" specialists.

Participate in a Mastermind group yourself and "benchmark" what works well or not so well; that is how you will know what to offer in your group. You will be able to hold exchanges with other participants so you can uncover their motivations and ambitions. You will become immersed, too, in the flow of activity that occurs inside of a Mastermind group.

Also, take part in events, be visible, take the lead on projects, communicate through your website, newsletter, and network of friends.

Invite People to Your Group!

People like it when you give them certain kinds of good attention. Also, make sure you emphasize the following when you write your invitation:

Mention how exclusive the group is! Invitees love to be treated like VIP's.

Be entertaining, in a creative kind of way! Everyone loves to be seduced by something that has an entertaining, fascinating, and dynamic dimension to it.

The group's intimate nature. Share with prospective members that the group's membership is restricted, and that, because of that, relationships that come about as a result of participation will be privileged. The group will be made up of people who share the same values, level of ambition, and respect for supporting and helping one another.

Be warm and towards those who come into the group: That kind of attitude is one of the reasons they decided to become a member. It is important for that each participant to rediscover herself/himself while pursuing her/his goals, and that she/he feels good while doing so. Remember that people are buying into the "reason" for what you do; they don't primarily think that they are "buying" what you will be doing to help them get to that point.

And finally, ask participants to bring someone that will be a plus factor for the group. The participants are sometimes in a better position to know who would be the best candidates for the group.

How Do You Make Your Mastermind Group Attractive to Potential Participants?

The idea is to come up with a group of people who come from totally different business sectors, but who might have the same kind of clients. Nobody competes with anybody else, even though the Mastermind's intention is to come up with a group that wants to rise up the ladder, as it develops cooperation; so that it will catch people's eye.

How Is This Done?

The idea is to instill motivation in people and create synergy; therefore, it is appropriate to choose points of commonality between the different participants, on the level of their individual identities, not just on the level of what they do for a living. Diversity will allow a greater richness when it comes to exchanges; collective intelligence will be in evidence at meetings. During the recruitment process, imagine what it will be like spending one day per month with participants. The way you feel at that moment is an important indicator.

A Scale for Selecting the People for Your Mastermind Group

Imagine a scale on which competency and excellence, when it comes to professional activity, is plotted. Only choose people who are, more or less, a couple of levels above you and the entire group. If some people become too advanced to be included on this scale, they should not remain in the group. Those individuals are, in effect, those who contribute the most to the group; but they don't get enough back from it. Let's remember that the goal of the group is for everyone to make gains from the relationships that are played out inside of it.

Who Should Be Chosen?

We recommend that you take a careful look at every candidate who comes to you so you can decide if you want to offer her/him a trial run of two or three meetings. Afterwards, her/his entry into the group can be approved through a vote.

5.4 Acceptance or Rejection of a Candidate

From Candidate to Member

Accepting a new member into a group is something that the group does together. Let's recall that there is a procedure that is used to determine if a candidate will be allowed to join.

* She/He is vetted as a candidate.

* She/He has accepted and participated in an interview with the facilitator.

* Her/His candidacy has been presented to the group, which has given the green light for a trial meeting for the candidate in question.

Therefore, it is up to the facilitator to support her/him by creating optimal conditions that will allow her/him to feel at ease, and so that she/he will be able to integrate the group's principles, goals, and rules and find a place in it.

Preliminary Phone Interview

This phone interview is ground zero for anybody who thinks that they might want to join the group. It is the starting point for any candidate. The facilitator will, at that time:

* Give a detailed explanation of the basis and form of a Master-mind group.

* Give explicit details about the group's special mindset, as well as about the rules for its functioning.

* Ask the candidate to fill out a candidate information sheet, as well as a special questionnaire. That is how the facilitator can come to an understanding about her/his motivations and goals and assess her/his capacity for commitment, in the service of the group.

The Interview

If the telephone interview is conclusive, the facilitator will propose a physical meeting. If the candidate is reluctant to move it will be a bad sign on her/his ability to be available later on for the group. It will be a question of evaluating the objectives of the candidate, her/his personality, her/his ambitions in terms of progress of business or leadership, and her/his motivations to integrate into the group.

We Recommend, At the Time of the Interview, and Before the First Meeting, That You...

Ask candidates to submit a CV or a description of their professional path up till now to you, so that the other members will be able to read it before the first meeting. Two personal references should also be submitted so that it can be verified that the candidate in question is an ethical individual. We also suggest that, during the course of the face-to-face interview, you get to know this possible future participant, and that you ask her/him questions so you can evaluate and come to a better understanding about her/his commitments and desires. The candidate should also fill out a questionnaire on which she/he will be asked to describe her/his motivations (see below).

Some Ideas for Questions

* What are you going to contribute to this Mastermind group?

* What about life brings you joy?

* What inspired your actions today? What makes you passionate?

* Do you have a personal or professional vision or mission?

* What are your goals one, five, ten years from now?

* How are you going to find the time to participate in our Mastermind group?

* Can you get involved ?

* How far do you want to advance in your business, so you can move up to a higher level?

* Do you feel you will be able to contribute to the group and ask for help at the same time?

* What are the skills, abilities, and knowledge that you think you can offer the group?

* Etc.

Those questions will allow you to evaluate the candidates' personalities, so you can determine if they seem as if they will be compatible with those of the other group members.

Group Validation

If the group hasn't developed the necessary maturity to make an appropriate decision about the individual in question, the facilitator will have to decide whether she/he will be accepted as a new member.

If the Mastermind group has the necessary maturity (which can be as soon as it is created), and if it uses collective intelligence, each member's opinion about the candidate will be important. Once the candidate has gone through her/his trial session, the facilitator will ask the others for their opinion.

* - The group will then vote. A unanimous vote is needed for the candidate to be accepted. The facilitator, generally speaking, arranges two different interviews, carried out by two different people, to validate the vote.

* - Only strong objections are taken into account and discussed before coming to a decision about whether to allow a candidate to join.

* - Or the facilitator will make the decision on her/his own, after she/he finds out the participants' opinion.

In the event of any doubt, the candidate might be invited back to participate in other meetings. If he/she end up being accepted, the group celebrates the acquisition of this new resource.

What Should Be Done If a Participant Does Not Seem to Be or Is no Longer Engaging with the Group?

First Indications

* She/He takes on no kind of responsibility and shares no feedback.

* She/He frequently changes her/his goals.

* She/he makes no significant progress.

* She/He takes action at the wrong time. She/He doesn't know how to prioritize tasks and/or projects.

Her/His Participation in the Group

* She/He does not engage in discussions with the group or the facilitator.

* She/He desires to leave the group before the end of the scheduled session.

* She/he doesn't show up for meetings.

* She/He doesn't participate in forums.

* She/He doesn't respond to e-mails or phone messages.

Emotional Signs

* She/He accuses the group environment and the group members for delays in getting things accomplished, and for every failure, etc.

* She/He does not re-evaluate things, nor does she/he take on any responsibility for that.

* She/He procrastinates and sabotages the work that she/he is supposed to be doing.

How Can She/He Be Helped?

It is important to remind her/him of the group's context and to keep the goals that she/he said she/he had when she/he first showed up in mind; also, about what she/he agreed to, and about the goals that she/he should be pursuing.

Lend support to her/him. Tell her/him that it is normal to have some periods when she/he will have some doubts. Help her/him divide her/his goals up. Spend a bit of time with her/him so that she/he can find her/his enthusiasm all over again. Ask the group to support her/him, too.

5.5 Rejection of a Candidate

How to reject and/or invite a Participant Who Does Not Fit in the Group to Leave

The facilitator might decide that it is better not to allow a certain candidate to come into her/his Mastermind group or that she/he should ask an individual who has placed herself/himself in a marginal position to leave. Those moments will, in all likelihood, be just as uncomfortable for her/him as they will be for the candidate who is being rejected, or for the participant who is about to leave; but it is better to reject a candidate or to ask a participant to leave, rather than have individuals in the group who don't have suitable personalities for it, or keep a person in it who no longer actively participates in the group's activities.

The facilitator, at the time of the rejection, should offer some constructive feedback to the candidate in question; she/he should do that in a clear, respectful, and sensitive way. It is a matter of ethical behavior and transparency. It is important for the candidate to understand why she/he wasn't accepted.

The reasons can be evidence-based:

* There could be some individuals in the group who are involved in the same activity that she/he is, so harmful competition could take place between those group members.

* The group might decide that it is complete the way it is, and therefore, does not want to bring in a new member.

* The candidate's project might not seem all that challenging or ambitious.

* The facilitator might not view the candidate's personality, as she/he has perceived it, as fitting in with those of the other group members.

* Or other evidence-based reasons.

The facilitator might propose that the rejected candidate or participant join another facilitator's group, or that she/he join one of her/his other groups, if she/he leads several.

The facilitator will inform the group about decisions that have been made: about the rejection of certain candidates, the departure of certain participants, and about those who are going to be allowed to join. This information will be followed by a process of inclusion for the new arrival, or one of exclusion for the person who is going to be leaving the group.

5.6 Are There obstacles to the Mastermind Group Participation?

Frankly speaking, those of us who are in Mastermind groups are real fans of them. So when we have to address the issue of blocks, when it comes to Mastermind group participation, it requires a great deal of effort. We need to remember the responses of people who never imagined that they would participate in a Mastermind group.

The benefits that come from participating in a Mastermind group seem so obvious to us that the objections you might come up with against it would not seem all that well-founded in comparison. That is not to say that there is no way that some of them are. But as far as we are concerned, the greatest "risk" that comes about from participating in a Mastermind group is that of succeeding more rapidly!

We have identified four kinds of doubts that hinder involvement in a Mastermind group. People who decide that there is no way that they are going to get involved in one are subject to the following four types of doubt:

1 – **Doubts in relation to the group:** The participant might have a fear of
being judged, of committing herself/himself to taking action, of being confronted, and fear of the group, because of a lack of confidence when she/he is confronted by people she/he doesn't know…

2 – **Doubts about the method:** That is to say, about its added value, its return on her/his investment, and its pertinence, which often comes about because of erroneous representations of the Mastermind group, and a certain kind of ignorance in relation to it.

3 – **Doubts about the facilitator:** That is to say, about her/his credibility, competence, or personal ethics.

4 – **Doubts related to herself/himself:** That is to say, about her/his availability, the necessary level of commitment, whether she/he has the financial means to participate, the desire/ability to learn, and enough self-esteem.

We offer responses to those doubts below. They represent the meat and potatoes of the initial contact with a future participant. You should, if necessary, be capable of reassuring the person with whom you are talking.

SELF-EVALUATION SURVEY:
AM I READY TO PARTICIPATE IN A MASTERMIND GROUP?

The following is a self-evaluation survey. It will help you determine if you are a suitable candidate for joining a Mastermind group. Rate yourself from 1 to 9, where 1 is very low or "not at all" and 9 is a strong agreement:

1 – I'm afraid that other people might find out what I might say during Mastermind sessions.

    1   2   3   4   5   6   7   8   9

2 – I'm afraid to be vulnerable while face-to-face with the group: that is to say, I'm afraid to talk about my doubts and my mistakes. I'm afraid of being judged and of the way the others will look at me.

    1   2   3   4   5   6   7   8   9

3 – I fear that my ideas will be stolen.

    1   2   3   4   5   6   7   8   9

4 – I fear that I might end up wasting my time.

    1   2   3   4   5   6   7   8   9

5 – I'm afraid that it will cost too much.

    1   2   3   4   5   6   7   8   9

6 – I'm afraid that I will not be able to follow through on my commitments.

    1   2   3   4   5   6   7   8   9

7 – I'm afraid that I might not learn all that much.

    1   2   3   4   5   6   7   8   9

8 – I'm afraid that I might spread myself too thin because I belong to other groups.

    1   2   3   4   5   6   7   8   9

9 – I'm afraid that I will put more into it than what I get out of it.

    1   2   3   4   5   6   7   8   9

10 – I'm afraid that the work involved might be a bit too much like therapy.

  1   **2**   **3**   **4**   **5**   **6**   **7**   **8**   **9**

11 – I'm afraid that this group might end up being just another kind of useless training.

  1   **2**   **3**   **4**   **5**   **6**   **7**   **8**   **9**

12 – I'm afraid that the people who are not familiar with my kind of business activity will not be able to help me.

  1   **2**   **3**   **4**   **5**   **6**   **7**   **8**   **9**

13 – The group reminds me of Alcoholics Anonymous.

  1   **2**   **3**   **4**   **5**   **6**   **7**   **8**   **9**

14 – I'm afraid that it will be of no use because people have no control over what might happen afterwards.

  1   **2**   **3**   **4**   **5**   **6**   **7**   **8**   **9**

15 – I'm afraid that it might be just another thing put out there by a consultant, just another new method.

  1   **2**   **3**   **4**   **5**   **6**   **7**   **8**   **9**

16 – I'm afraid that I might not have the right skills to participate.

  1   **2**   **3**   **4**   **5**   **6**   **7**   **8**   **9**

We have come up with answers to these blocks. We hope that they will give enough reassurance to those who are undecided, so they can at least allow themselves to try out the experience of a Mastermind group.

1 – I'm afraid that what might be said in the Mastermind group will harm my business' image.

Confidentiality is one of the things that participants are supposed to observe. It is a part of the group's framework, and each person must agree to it in writing. It only happens very rarely, but if one of the members doesn't respect the obligation to keep what is said in the group confidential, she/he ends up being excluded from the group.

2 – I'm afraid that I will feel vulnerable while I'm in front of the group.

Trust and an ability to care about others are qualities that are needed to join a Mastermind group. They reflect the mindset that its participants are required to have. The facilitator needs to guarantee that. The selection process allows her/him to seek out those kinds of participants. The facilitator should pay close attention to that. Some other participants will, in all likelihood, have the same kind of fear, so it will be possible for everyone to grow together, when it comes to that. It is important for the facilitator to reassure the person who aspires to be a member by stating that the other participants are in the same boat.

3 – I'm afraid that someone will steal my ideas (trust).

The ability to trust makes up part of the selection criteria for a Mastermind group. The process of candidate selection allows the facilitator to choose people who are not involved in other group activities, at the same time. However, no idea can be fully protected. It only has value when it turns into something concrete. Exposing ideas to other participants will allow them to be improved upon, and to be more effective after they are carried out. Ideas come to us and to other people through exchanges that promote collective intelligence. An idea grows better in the minds in which it wasn't created in the first place. Therefore, we have a complete and total interest in making use of collective intelligence, which is the primary Mastermind process, so that our ideas can grow, by taking advantage of how they resonates with the rest of the participants. The development of ideas requires trust between the Mastermind members.

In a Mastermind group, "if two people have a dollar each and they swap their dollars, each of them is still left with only one dollar. If two people swap their ideas, each of them will be left with at least two ideas". So one cannot possess an idea. A facilitator can, however, have participants sign a confidentiality agreement that covers projects that the group might address.

The exchange of ideas gives members the opportunity to see how they resonate with those of the rest of the group. That is how new ideas can emerge; ideas which will be even more powerful. An idea is only powerful when implemented; keeping it in the back of a drawer does not benefit anyone or anything at all.

Confidentiality and trust are a couple of key elements when it comes to the emergence of brilliant ideas! It is up to the facilitator to guarantee that these key factors takes place!

4 – I'm afraid that I might waste my time/I'm afraid that the group might take up too much of my time.

All participants share concerns about the amount of time that is devoted to a group, since each one of them wants the sessions to be effective. But that commitment of time happens to be one of the components that makes Mastermind groups successful. The time frame for Mastermind sessions shared from the start. Each participant is made aware of the number of meetings that will take place, and at what times, and that she/he has to commit to being on time to said meetings. The facilitator guarantees that the group will be carried out inside of this time-based framework, which can be modified if that is what a majority of participants want. Everything is carried out so that the meetings fit seamlessly into the schedule. The goal of the Mastermind group is to be efficient. An important principle, when it comes to efficiency, is that one has to know how to "waste" (or rather, invest) some time in order to gain some later on.

The formats that we have proposed allow meetings to be planned and included on the group schedule well in advance. The work to be carried out has to do with participants' projects or businesses. As far as the group facilitator's own business issues are concerned, the Mastermind group experience offers her/him the opportunity to attend to them; that is to say, the group is of use for her/his own project, too. Paradoxically, distancing oneself from one's own issues makes it possible to be more effective when it comes to serving others' needs. But that allows the facilitator to develop, even more, her/his identity as a leader. Some meetings are held online, which means that they are not too much of a burden in terms of schedules. Mastermind meetings are to be managed like other professional meetings. Time is invested, not wasted. The time that is invested prepares one for the future. Participating in a Mastermind group allows one to advance along a new path so that one can make a larger leap. It also allows one to stand back, with the help of caring peers, and see where any shortcuts to success might be.

5 – I'm afraid that the group might cost a lot.

It all depends on what you are comparing the cost of a Mastermind group to and on what you expect to get from it. If your participation allows you to learn, gain time, have access to information that you wouldn't have access to otherwise, move a step up, or even make a quantum leap, then the cost probably does not seem all that high. Moreover, a high fee tends to make each participant become all the more engaged. Mastermind groups should not be primarily thought of as an expense, but as investments. They are opportunities to speed up the attainment of success and the desired results. They allow one to stand back and look at her/his situation in other kinds of ways.

Most facilitators allow potential participants to carry out a trial so they can see how the Mastermind group in question works. This trial period should allow every participant the opportunity to form her/his own opinion about the cost-effectiveness of participation in the group. It will also be beneficial to ask the members of the group what they get from their participation. Does it have to do with the money they have paid? Is that why they come back?

6 – I'm afraid that I will not be able to follow through on my commitments.

The purpose of Mastermind processes are to help participants follow through on their commitments. It is important to actually measure a member's capacity to make a commitment, not only for you, but also for the group, which is there to help members succeed in a caring way (but without any complacency).

7 – I'm afraid I might not learn all that much.

Can one truly believe that, in this world, which constantly changes, one can NOT allow herself/himself to assimilate new knowledge and then have a vision that is unique? Nowadays, businesses need to innovate; and innovation, by definition, refers to something that one has never known about! Einstein said that imagination is more important than knowledge. That's even truer today. A Mastermind group is not a venue for training; Instead, it is a way of using several minds so that every participant can be served, and so that each person moves in the direction of her/his stated goal. However, a person who really thinks that she/he knows more than the others perhaps really shouldn't be in a Mastermind group, since it is one in which peers know only as much as the next guy, and nothing more.

8 – I'm afraid that I will spread myself too thin since I already belong to other groups (e.g., associations for entrepreneurs, Club Agile, CJD, Germe...)

These groups and associations also extend their offer of services in a way that employs principles that are more like those of collective intelligence, and less like those of training. They use, for example, co-development groups, and then, in no time at all, their members might get involved in Mastermind groups. Keep participating in those other groups. The Mastermind group is not in competition with them—they complement them.

At the time of one of our interviews, a manager was doubtful about the added value of the Mastermind group because he was already working with a coach who was helping him with his business projects. Here is what he said: "I showed up with my issue, thinking I had looked at it from every possible angle. I only wanted an outside opinion about the different solutions I had come up with. I was really bowled over by the high quality of opinions and the pertinence of the advice, which my colleagues, who had tested them out through their experiences, offered me. I tip my hat to them for having found a new solution for me. which seems so obvious to me tonight."

9 – I'm afraid that I will put more into it than what I will get out of it.

Sometimes people actually both give and ask for a lot. However, the facilitator is there to create a balance between contributions and what is taken from them for each participant. She/He is able to evaluate participants' satisfaction, and if necessary, bring the issue up with the group so that it can take a position and reconsider how it functions. Therefore, you should feel free to share your feelings with both the facilitator and the group. The facilitator makes every effort to make sure the each participant's status is similar, so that each of them can get support that will be powerful enough, and so that they are satisfied with the added value they have received.

10 – I'm afraid that it will be too much like therapy. I don't want to "naked" in front of everyone

A Mastermind group has absolutely nothing to do with psychological therapy; it has nothing to do with baring one's soul in front of everybody else. If you join a Mastermind group, that means that you should be ready to be confronted with new ideas. People are there because they are interested in their futures, not because of what has happened in the past, which is the case with therapy. A Mastermind group is interested, in one word, in "how" (an orientation towards the future) and not in "why" (an orientation towards the past). A Mastermind group is not the least bit like a therapy group. It is a process where colleagues discuss cases as equals. Being non-judgmental is one of its fundamental rules. On the other hand, participants should have a sufficiently open mind so they can give, receive, and ask for constructive, useful, and sometimes even disturbing feedback. Anyway, how can one ever progress and modify her/his project if all she/he ever hears is what he/she wants to hear?

11 – I'm afraid that it will be just one more useless training group.

The biggest problem that one runs into with training groups is that they look at things in a restricted, inflexible kind of way. When training goes on, a lot of people end up saying to themselves, "but it doesn't work that way for me." The Mastermind group isn't at all like a training group. Participants in a Mastermind group are practitioners who share their experiences, successes, and mistakes; they contribute advice and an outside point of view. It is something very different than training groups and there is more added value for business leaders because of that. The Mastermind group emphasizes personal and practical solutions.

12 – I'm afraid that people who are not familiar with my kind of business activity will not be able to offer me anything, due to its highly specific nature.

It is exactly this diversity of participants that contributes to the Mastermind group's high added value. Each person shares her/his vision, experiences, area of expertise, and different networks... The group will never focus on things that are specific to a participant's profession, but on processes that are common to all businesses, on how the project is being carried out, and on the development of business leadership.

13 – It reminds me of Alcoholics Anonymous.

Alcoholics Anonymous groups have been in existence since 1935. They were created because of a need to share like experiences and get beyond one's difficulties, specifically, those that have to do with abstaining from alcohol, which is a truly formidable challenge. And their method, in part based on co-responsibility, mutual help, emotional engagement, and the power of the group, has proved to the very effective. So we respect that venerable institution. But no... A Mastermind group isn't at all like an Alcoholics Anonymous group. It is instead a group for future-oriented business leaders who are united in a common cause.

14 – I'm afraid that the group will be of no use because one can't change whatever might happen afterwards.

One can, however, add things to her/his repertoire so she/he can increase the amount of things she/he can play around with. Even though she/he still has the same repertoire, she/he has a lot more possibilities when it comes to accomplishing things. It has to do with seeing things from another point of view, of thinking about your vision of the world in another way, etc. It is a real strategic advantage. But someone might truly believe that she/he cannot change, no matter what, when she/he believes that the Mastermind group hasn't been created for her/him, in particular. One of its prerequisites for being a participant in a Mastermind group is that one has to be convinced that she/he can make rapid progress, grow as a human being and professionally, by having contact with the other members of the group. She/he has to also accept the fact that she/he will have to take a long, hard look at herself/himself.

15 – I'm afraid that it might be just another thing put out there by a consultant, just another new method.

People have heard the same thing said about business coaching. Nowadays, coaching is solidly anchored in the practices of managers, business leaders, and entrepreneurs. The Mastermind group is a process that was described by Napoleon Hill in 1920. It is a process that has proved to be effective.

We don't think that Mastermind groups are just one other method, since they respond to a great many issues, using the principles, which have hardly been exploited, of collective intelligence. One progresses more quickly when she/he works on her/his own (coaching) but goes farther when she/he works with others (collective coaching/Mastermind groups).

16 – I'm afraid that I might not have the right skills to participate to the group.

The attributes that one should have for participation in a Mastermind group are those that are essentially human: a desire to help peers, a positive attitude when confronted with life and its challenges, a desire to take on ambitious challenges, respect for others, common sense, an ability to do some self-analysis… Every other skill that has to do with technique is learned. A Mastermind group is a really good place to learn all of that, through the example and actions of the other participants. Moreover, lack of skills in certain areas allows one to ask experts candid questions about a specific issue, which brings about progress in that area. Such questions allow the expert to reformulate, synthesize, and make her/his demonstrations more simple, at the same time that they are more powerful. Einstein said that if someone has really understood something, he/she should be able to explain it to a six-year old child.

When You Are Confronted by Doubts that People Might Have About Your Mastermind Group

- Doubts about the group, the facilitator, and the methods employed

Let the person know, as clearly as possible, that you are asking the above questions at the same time that you are reassuring her/him about how the Mastermind group structure protects and engages each participant, and that that would apply to her/him, too. The easiest thing to do is to talk to her/him about all of that.

- Self-doubts

Don't force the person to participate in the group, especially if, after all of the information you have shared with her/him, she/he still doubts herself/ himself when it comes to her/his availability and desire/ability to learn from the experience. Remember that she/he is the expert when it comes to her/his own life, and she/he knows what is appropriate in her/his case; she/he will know if it's the right time to join. Wanting her/him to join the group, at all costs, could be very counterproductive and could turn into a burden for the whole group, at a later time.

It might seem like we are describing Mastermind groups as if they are some kind of panacea, the ultimate solution to every problem, a "magical magic trick". That, obviously, is not the case, and let us say, in all frankness, that some Mastermind groups do not work out and do not survive their first few months of existence. The usual reason for that is lack of experience on the part of the facilitator when it comes to managing the group dynamics of building trust, facilitating communication, and creating a generative field among all participants.

The group will not be able to function if the facilitator isn't able to deal with different personalities and difficult situations in a positive way; if she/ he goes along with keeping people who don't, or who no longer have a place in the group; if she/he does not maintain a high level of added value when it comes to the length of the group session and creative tension; if she/he does not create enough instances where participants take action, or does not maintain a group structure that is clear enough, or a vision that is ambitious enough. Sometimes, she/he is not sufficiently committed to serve the interests of participants, or is just not warm enough. The generative capacity of the group becomes diminished when members of the group have not understood the meaning or the implications of their participation in the group.

5.7 What Participants Actually Say

At the same time that we have been writing this book and carrying out a few interviews at different places throughout the world, we have given six business managers the opportunity to have the experience of being in Mastermind group so that they can contribute some feedback.

Likewise, in November of 2016, at the 4th congress on collective intelligence, in Avignon, 33 participants came to our Mastermind workshop so they could experience a hot seat session for an hour. We are going to share their feedback with you.

It is easy for consultants to become enthusiastic about new tools that seem full of promise. There is a risk, however, of becoming disconnected from the needs of clients and of the people with whom one is concerned. That is why we took the initiative to undertake this experiment; we wanted to gather our participants' reactions so it could be verified that the hot seat isn't just some kind of "consultants' trick", and that what we experienced in our group has also been experienced in other groups.

A Proposal

The proposal, for the managers, was for them to go in for the Mastermind group experience twice, for three hours at a time, spaced three weeks apart, concentrating only on the love/hot seat experience. It was exactly the same for the workshop that was part of the collective intelligence conference, except the experience took place only once, and for one hour only.

Rolling Out of the Session

The Managers

Of the six managers who were invited, only four agreed to undergo the Mastermind group experience. One of them wasn't interested in it; one other manager was only available on one of the two dates. And for the record, after the first afternoon with just the four managers, the latter expressed the desire to continue with just four because something good had happened between them, so it seemed to them that it would be hard to have a new person come in after that (that was interesting to us, because we always think about how to have new members come into Mastermind groups). Three of the four managers went on the hot seat for about an hour and a half; the only one who didn't had the opportunity to present his case once, and then another time, at the time of the second session.

For the Mastermind Workshop in Avignon

We created, with the 33 participants at the workshop, three circles of 11 people each. Each circle gathered around someone who had accepted our proposal to bring in their case, and who had been designated to go onto the hot seat. Speaking about an actual personal problem to 11 people whom you have just met seemed as if it were going to be a tricky situation for our workshop. The results, however, were quite positive.

Testimonials (for reasons of confidentiality, we have suppressed the names of the participants)

For the Managers (contacted by cold e-mail)

First Three-Hour Session

"I showed up with my issue, thinking that I had looked at it from every possible angle. All that I wanted was an outside opinion about the different solutions I had come up with. I was, in return, really impressed by the high quality of the opinions and by the pertinence of the advice that my colleagues, who had tested them out through their experiences. I tip my hat to them for having found a new solution for me, which seems so obvious to me tonight. Besides the pleasure that I got out of the shared exchanges about the two issues, I sincerely thank all three of them for the invaluable help they gave me. I, for sure, didn't waste my time that afternoon..."

"That afternoon's experience confirms, for me, how we can gain so much by all of us opening up to one another when there is trust and respect. Ours is a really great task, and it carries a great deal of responsibility with it."

"It is a task that instills fear in me because it seems solitary and as if it might lead to excesses when it comes to power and the ego. I am learning, along with you, and along with others, that when they go hand in hand with humility, the opening up of the mind, and an alert kind of awareness, make for a beautiful path in life. I'm convinced that we need this kind of regard for one another so that we can get out of the ruts that each one of us gets bogged down in, and so that we can then gain in energy and strength. I am very happy to have shared this time with you, and rejoice at the thought of the next meeting, even though you have set the bar high."

"... I am very happy about this experience, which seemed to me like a calm interlude, during which I sought consultation in relation to a really big issue, which, as far as I am concerned, should have remained a minor one, but which, in spite of me, has run over me like a tidal wave. At first I was, amazed by how serious you were about listening to me, and by the importance you lent to the personal agony I felt about having to make a decision. I came to feel reassured, later on, by the diversity of your concrete, pertinent ideas, which are finally accessible."

"The group's fraternal kind of structure, although it's one that does not lend itself to complacency, has been extremely important. I have come back feeling lighter, but also with a good dose of determination. Thanks to every one of you for that."

"It was a really great afternoon. It was a bit cool in the room, but what heat there was in the group! Collective intelligence gets all of its meaning from what's going on here. Thanks for the shared trust; I think that this experience has also brought us a little closer to one another. Bravo! The bar is high, but because of the calming, constructive exchanges, I am (almost) no longer afraid about our next meeting..."

After the Second Three-Hour Session (the end of the experience)
Here is the synthesis of hot seat participants' responses.

In three words, what benefits have you gotten out of your participation in the Mastermind group?

* *A feeling of momentum, bonding, experimentation.*
* *The ability to trust others, courage, and self-confidence.*
* *Some advice, because of my confidence in others, and because of the exchanges.*
* *Calm exchanges, a desire to help others, trust among peers.*

What did you notice while you were in the group?

* *The pertinence of the advice.*
* *The shared desire to be there for the rest.*
* *The sincerity of my three accomplices.*
* *The capacity that everyone had for going out of our comfort zones, even when it was truly uncomfortable.*
* *The need to emerge from our own space.*
* *The strength of the collective.*
* *How difficult it is to keep a proper distance when one is confronting their problem alone, or in relation to people who are also involved in it.*
* *The capacity of every person to help you and to become mobilized, so they can give you caring advice.*
* *The finesse with which the group analyzed my issue. My intent*

was to submit a problem which could, at first glance, might have looked like something hypersensitive, or even bland or boring. I didn't hear anyone pass judgment—far from it. The summary that all three of them gave of my problem did not upset me.

How should things progress? And what are your recommendations for taking the group to a higher level?

* To go after the experience.

* I don't know. Each step really bowls me over. I am never all that motivated. But I come out of this experience super convinced, and in top condition, mentally speaking.

* Nothing should be changed: A coach seems to be necessary, as well as a group of people with whom you feel safe.

* Do some of the hot seats over again… And why not do some new activities.

Share three words that describe your experience

* Enriching, warm, reassuring.

* Inspiring, warm, effective.

* Destabilizing, useful, clears the air.

* Amazing! You feel like you are no longer alone, like everyone is sincere.

According to you, what qualities does a person need to have to take part in a Mastermind group?

* She/He should be involved, sincere, non-judgmental, and exercise humility.

* She/He should show respect for others, be altruistic, as well as experienced at life.

* She/He should be transparent, trust the others in the group, and be open-minded.

* She/He should have a great deal of confidence in the other members, be transparent, and have the desire to share.

What, according to you, would be the ideal frequency and duration of a Mastermind group?

* 9 months, with a meeting held every six weeks.

* I have no idea. It seems to me that two meetings is already a big commitment. That being said, we have already planned to meet again.

* *Six afternoons, over a period of nine months, and then possibly start all over again, after that.*

* Every two to three months…

Bearing in mind its added value, what should the cost for participating in a Mastermind group of this frequency and duration be?

* *I don't have any idea.*

* *1,000 euro per half day, to be split up among the members of the group.*

* *I don't have any idea, all the more so because we've only been experienced just a little bit of it, at this point…*

What, according to you, in just a few words, should be the role of the facilitator in a Mastermind group?

* *To reassure, re-focus members, take them off center.*

* *To sort things out, re-focus members, advise.*

* *To maintain the group's scope, re-focus members, maximize the success of the experience.*

The following are the words of participants who took part in the workshop at the collective intelligence conference, after each of them went through the experience of the love/hot seat.

What can you tell us about your experience on the hot seat? How do you feel about it?

"First, I want to express my extreme gratitude for having gotten so much out of it, and for even what seemed like a lot of love. I felt like a lot of caring was going on. That really gives you a lot of confidence so you can say certain things that you otherwise might not. It opens the way to the formation of other perspectives. It's powerful; one comes up with a lot of solutions, and a lot of things become enabled, in certain areas. There are some things that we really talk about, and then you end up wondering why you didn't think of it earlier. A whole lot of things resonate. We feel that we are surrounded by a lot of resources and help, and that gives us confidence. That gives us the desire to act. You really get a lot out of it—One doesn't usually get that much caring or advice directed at her/him. One doesn't know how she/he could ever do anything to show her/his thanks to the others. I think that when one finds herself/himself in the position of being able to give advice, she/he wants to give back as much as she/he has received, and she/he wants the other to succeed as much as the rest of us do. That's the Mastermind principle. It's has to do with having total harmony in the group. And when one experiences that, it is a real energetic force and concrete support."

"It's an amazing, emotional, constructive experience. I received, in relation to the issue I was preoccupied with, in record time, and in a very pertinent way, information, and a certain amount of emotional stimuli which affected me a lot. It was like a collection of emotions, ideas, suggestions, and reasoning that led me to ask myself questions all over again. I reaped a great deal of benefits from all of that; the pertinence of it, and how quickly things were accomplished, really amazed me. What is truly amazing is the way people reacted, asked questions, and when they expressed their reactions. Each time, all that came from people who didn't know me but who nevertheless reflected, in a manner that was totally pertinent, one facet of me. Not only was it pertinent, but it was expressed in a way that was caring, and without any complacency. It is like a cocktail that I would not be able to describe in any other way than by saying that it is half-way between the thought, the impression, intuition, and feelings."

It made me feel very calm, and very creative, to see that creative structure, which seemed light and rich, at the same time. You leave with ideas, with an impression. The people who are there are willing to carry you on their shoulders as you go along your path. I think that it can stir you up, of course, that it can shake you up... But that's what you're there for."

"Within a very short time, because there's only one an hour, you discover all of the real power of the Mastermind method. It is a way of improving, in many respects, the project that has been brought in, and which, as a result, can be called into question, so that others can give advice, and then new paths can be opened up... The individual in question, quite naturally, presented his project to us, and we had seven minutes to bombard him with questions. It went by quickly. We had enough time to get to the bottom of things. We wanted to be on the love seat, too, because we also wanted to benefit from others' questions about our own projects."

Chapter 6

What Key Factors Lead to the Success of a Mastermind Group?

Looking at the formation of a Mastermind group from a systemic perspective, we can see that many factors come into play when launching the group. Attending to these factors will help support participants throughout the process, so they can achieve, and even exceed, the results that are expected by the group.

A Mastermind group is a unique and special gathering. If participants are expected to achieve excellence, then that intention should be reinforced at every step along the way. When the message is consistent, the Mastermind group will become a breeding ground for learning and for absolutely dazzling successes. Each step that is taken while a Mastermind group is taking place should then be thought of as an event, in its own right. The success of the group requires a significant amount of work on the part of everyone.

Integrating what we have learned from taking the *Facilitating Collective Intelligence* training with Robert Dilts, reading numerous articles and participating in our own Mastermind group, we want to share the key elements that we believe will ensure the success of a Mastermind group.

Keep in mind that the success of a Mastermind group comes, in particular, from its capacity to create a generative state. This requires the full participation of all group members in order to pool their brain power. That should lead to the creation of a group that produces results that are "greater than the sum of its parts."

Mastermind groups are an expression of generative collaboration. People gather together for the purpose of creating or generating something new and often surprising, something that will exceed the abilities of individuals on their own. It is something similar to what happens when an atom of oxygen and two of hydrogen join together to create water.

There are numerous negative factors, however, that can limit the learning and effectiveness of groups. These negative factors reduce the participants' abilities to be more productive, even when members try to work together, causing them to under perform.

The following limiting factors are drawn from an article, written by Dominque Oberlé, that appeared in the June 2016 edition of *Cerveau et Psycho1* They identify some of the blocks and obstacles that the facilitator should become familiar with so she/he can manage them:

* The bias of conformity, which leads people to adopt the point of view of the majority.

* The lack of a sharing of information, so that only one person in the possession of key knowledge.

* The bias of confirmation, which leads people to select and focus on only parts of the totality information that has been exchanged, based on how comfortable it makes them feel, and how much it confirms their own point of view.

---

1   Oberlé, Dominque, *Les clés de l'intelligence collective-Comment bien raisonner ensemble*, *Cerveau et Psycho*, June 2016, No. 78., p.44.

The ability of a group's participants to reflect honestly and authentically through debate (and not a weak compromise), on their own blocks and obstacles, such as those above, is necessary for the emergence of intelligent collective decisions.

And even when participants are not involved in the process of a collective decision-making, such as when the group is supporting a particular participant to act on something she/he wants to implement, it is still appropriate to keep those biases in mind, as they can affect the group member's ability to support one another.

As a result of our experience, we have identified the following five factors as being essential to a Mastermind group's success:

1. The "quality" of participants.
2. The facilitator's role.
3. The relational and generative fields of the group.
4. The taking of action.
5. A stimulating, protective framework for the group's good functioning.

6.1 The "Quality" of Participants

As mentioned previously, recruitment is a crucial step when it comes to ensuring the success of a Mastermind group. Before forming her/his group, the facilitator should reflect upon and define a clear, rigorous process for selecting its members.

Paradoxically, the group's members should be both homogeneous in some aspects and heterogeneous in others in order to be able to share, learn, evolve, and experience personal and professional growth together. For example, the group should be homogeneous with regard to the aspirations, ambitions and the professional successes of each member. It is important for each participant to share these intentions to be able to effectively give to and receive from the others. She/He should feel that her/his contribution is useful and that she/he is benefiting from the contributions of others.

As an example, a young self-promoter will, in all likelihood, be very interested in rubbing shoulders with experienced business managers who are heads of companies that have sales in the tens of millions. It is likely, however, that the experienced managers will not get the same kind of benefits from the experience that the self-promoter will.

At the same time, the group should be sufficiently heterogeneous as far as skills, professional paths, and frames of reference, so that there can be real diversity among its members. Under those circumstances, different members will complement one another and there will be a cross-fertilization of ideas.

No one in the group should agree with everybody else all of the time; each individual is responsible for her/his own decisions and for carrying out the actions that lead to her/his success. She/He gathers as many of the other Mastermindians' thoughts and proposals about how she/he might want to act as she/he can. The diversity of the participant's points of view is essential; it will lead participants to look from every angle, consider every option, and choose those that seem to offer the most promise of success.

Psychologist Anita Woolley, from Carnegie Mellon University in Pittsburgh, has shown that groups that bring together diverse cognitive styles are more effective than those in which the personalities are very similar. There's no need to have experts in order for a group to reach a high level of performance and be an example for others. But it is imperative for the group to bring together people who are curious, truly interested and invested in what is going on, have different kinds of knowledge, and who are going along different personal and professional paths.

Mastermind group members will be able to integrate different perspectives, develop resources and deploy new strategies by confronting their diverse ideas. The complexity of the situations that people join a Mastermind group in order to address requires more types of knowledge and skill that any one individual will possess. A the wealth of ideas emerges from bringing several minds together, creating a truly collective intelligence that can help everyone in the group.

That kind of diversity is a plus factor; but it is also a risk when one thinks about it from the point of view of different personalities. It is necessary for members of a group to have personalities that are at least minimally compatible. They also need to share certain values and principles that we will specify in the section on establishing the framework for operating a Mastermind group (see page 207).

What is essential for each participant is to be fully present, accept that she/he needs to reveal herself/himself as she/he actually is, share her/his experiences, receive feedback so she/he can progress toward her/his goals as a result of the variety of perspectives and ideas that are offered by the group.

In summary the facilitator should concentrate on creating a group that is both diverse and consistent among members.

6 .2 The Facilitator's Role

Like Otto Scharmer, who came up with Theory U, has pointed out, the success of an intervention depends on the inner state of the one who is doing it. That assumption is illustrative of the second element that is key to the success of a Mastermind group: the facilitator's role and attitude.

Each Mastermind group is unique, certainly because of the uniqueness of the members that make it up, but also because of the facilitator's personality and goals. The latter two elements lend a very specific color to her/his group.

As with all support techniques, tools and methods are necessary; but the group's success and its unique character depend fundamentally on the facilitator's consistency and her/his state of being.

It is also necessary for the facilitator to have her/his own vision, goals, mission, and role for her/his Mastermind group well defined. She/He should be clear as far as the "why" for the group. This includes what she/he intends to contribute to the group and its environment, and what she/he wants to get out of it for herself/himself. Does she/he want to diversify her/his business activity, develop a sales strategy, or allow third parties to benefit from a specialized, high-performance, powerful method? There are as many goals as there are facilitators; it's up to each of them to decide what they are.

She/He likewise needs to clarify the purpose for her/his Mastermind group and to whom it is more specifically addressed. For example, it can be meant for women who want to break through the glass ceiling, young entrepreneurs who are at least 30 years old, or senior managers who want to develop their businesses internationally...

If a Mastermind group is supposed to offer a platform where all of its members can achieve excellence, then this intention needs to be given as a clear and consistent message from the start by the one has who created it.

The facilitator should be aware of what kind of impact she/he will have, and how she/he can influence the group members' achievement of their goals. Her/His attitude should be as exemplary and consistent as possible so that she/he can motivate each one of them to assume a similar one. She/He must be daring enough to go beyond what her/his own barriers are and to get past anything that seems like a limitation.

Previous skill in organizing group activities, or in the coaching of teams, will, without a doubt, be an asset. One just can't "wing it" when it comes to that kind of role.

It is necessary, from our point of view, to be enthusiastic so you can infuse others with passion and desire, show "love" for other people, have a desire to contribute to their progress. It is also important to believe in them and in their potential without forcing anything on them.

In effect, the goals, objectives, implemented methods, and actions that are carried out are all up to the members; the facilitator should constantly make sure that she/he does not take that role away from them. In a Mastermind group, the facilitator and the participants are partners in a relationship and when it comes to action.

The participant is responsible for her/his own development and progress, as she/he interacts with herself/himself and the entire group; that ensures that everybody has a role that will guarantee each person's progress. The facilitator is responsible for making sure that the process runs smoothly and for managing the group's membership.

The support offered by the facilitator needs to support this mutual commitment. The facilitator, depending on the situation, should help to focus the group's interactions, summarize and synthesize group members' contributions and re-focus exchanges. She/He should remain as neutral and as objective as possible, and totally respect the confidentiality of exchanges. Finally, she/he sometimes has to act as a referee while, at the same time, enable confrontation and exchanges, which are sometimes contradictory, so that ideas and solutions can emerge. That is how participants will be able to carry out innovative actions.

Thus, the facilitator has a double responsibility:

1. One that is *relational* in nature, since she/he promotes human interactions. She/He must create and maintain motivation, trust, and a climate of openness in which group members can open up. The latter is fundamental to the achievement of the level of generativity that will differentiates Mastermind groups from other professional development methods.

2. One that is *operational*, since she/he sets up methods and creates processes. The facilitator ensures that the process go smoothly, and monitors each step. She/He also ensures that the Mastermind group will last for as long as it is supposed to, even beyond in-person encounters. It is essential for members to invest some time and energy between meetings. To that end, the facilitator can propose some phone conferences, in the interim, and access to a collaborative platform so that members of the group develop a strong sense of belonging and a feeling of solidarity, so that each person can be a resource for others.

6.3 Relational and Generative Fields

We know that among the basic elements that allow for the success of teams, the human one is the most important. This has to do with the ability of individuals to form and maintain bonds, and to cooperate and develop synergies that will allow the team to perform at a high level.

J.S. Brown, a manager at Rank Xerox, illustrates that idea quite well: "Everything that is accomplished here is the result of collaboration; that is the case everywhere in today's high-tech world. There are no more solitary geniuses. Even Edison was a brilliant leader of a team. We, in the first place, manage human capital: The ideas don't come out of a single brain but are the result of an exchange, a collaboration, in the greatest sense of the word."

These same collaborative principles obviously apply to the functioning of Mastermind groups. It is through acknowledging each other's differences, and reinforcing an aptitude for identifying and leveraging synergies, that the participants will be able to develop a high-level relational and generative field amongst themselves.

Those fields rely on three factors that have already been described—resonance, synergy, and emergence. It is from combining these three phenomena that a generative field is created. It is through the quality of interactions and relationships between people that this field becomes transformed into a generative, creative one—a field that is filled with possibilities that are ready to be turned into reality.

The quality of these fields is important because, if high, they strengthen generative collaboration and allow the individual intelligence of the group members to multiply. Certain individuals' talents are a catalyst for developing talents in others; ideas bounce off one another, solutions appear on the horizon, and the final result greatly exceeds that the individuals could achieve working separately: "The whole is greater than the sum of its parts".

Chuck Steele, an ex-trainer for the Pittsburgh Pirates, confided the following to Daniel Goleman, a PhD psychologist who teaches at Harvard: "As a mathematician, I always believed that the whole is equal to the sum of its parts. And when I became a trainer, I noticed that the whole is NEVER equal to the sum of its parts. It is either larger or not as large, depending on how the individuals who make it up work together."

Then what is it that makes a team or a group get better results than just the addition of team members? What makes it becomes more innovative and higher performing? What is it that allows it to reach the highest level? Certain individuals like Napoleon Hill, Robert Dilts, and Olivier Zara describe this collective ability as a superior kind of intelligence that transcends the individuals in the group, at the same time that it respects each individuals who are present. It is an exponential intelligence that could never be achieved by just a single person.

Applied to a Mastermind group, the sharing of a collective goal creates an environment that allows participants to gather information and ideas that they would have never been able to find on their own, in spite of their individual experiences and skills. A special kind of creativity, then, is at work between the members. Moreover, it's not all that rare for Mastermindians to have the same idea at the same time. The quality of communication and the listening is more intense and is played out by going beyond the words. That goes to the heart of what is actually happening.

The explanation for this phenomenon resides, for Daniel Goleman, in the nature of the relationships between members of the group and of the emotional chemistry that bonds them. He says that "a superb intellect and technical talent do not, in and of themselves, make a great team". He continues b pointing out: "Groups that take pleasure in working together, collaborators that appreciate one another, who know how to joke around with one another and share the good times, possess emotional capital that allows them to not only to excel during periods when they are prosperous, but also to get through difficult phases. Groups that haven't figured out or that have not been able to establish these bonds run a greater risk of paralysis and dysfunction, even disintegration, if they fall under pressure."

Using that as a starting point, one can understand the importance of using emotions in an effective way during a Mastermind meeting.

The word "emotion" comes from the Latin motere, which means "to move"; its first letter, "e", is indicative of "movement towards the outside". So etymologically speaking, emotions are not passive feelings but instead trigger movement. Unfortunately, when we are in school, we are not taught how to recognize and use emotions as effectively as we can, and the self-willed use of them is still not all that accepted in the professional world. On the contrary, it is often said that emotions are embarrassing, potentially harmful and should be suppressed. We believe that, because emotions play a central role when it comes to how we function, ignoring their positive power demonstrates a lack of insight.

Our emotions prepare us to act. To think of our thought processes as the only things that dictate our actions is a mistake. Our emotions guide us, in a significant way, as we make our decisions so that we can accomplish things. They help us, more specifically, to confront difficult and sometimes dangerous situations, accomplish courageous actions, re-establish contact with other people, develop powerful bonds, and reinforce our energy and motivation.

To be effective a Mastermind group needs to focus on the appropriate use of emotions and to fully integrate it with the capacity for rational understanding. They are both essential levers that will make the difference when it comes to the strength of the bonds between Mastermindians, the pertinence of proposals, and the strength of commitments that will be made by participants.

During a Mastermind meeting, all emotions, whether expressed or not, are welcome. Destabilizing emotions, such as shame or guilt, for example, need to be acknowledged, accepted and given a place so that they do not become the proverbial "elephant in the room ". We have also said that a Mastermind group allows one to make progress as a human being. And we guarantee that better management of emotions will help participants to progress when it comes to their ability to deal with challenging situations. Supporting the group to deal with awkward situations, doubts, dissatisfactions, concerns, or fears can help them get beyond memories that are still dogging them in the present.

The facilitator should make a great deal of effort to create an emotional framework that will allow each person to express herself/himself in a totally secure way. This framework is built from the trust that emerges between group members. Some people are able to express and deal with their emotions more easily than others. They can serve as an example and "model" that for the others, opening the way so that other participants can learn to let go and get beyond what's blocking them, and exceed their current limits. Being a Mastermindian means that you agree to confront yourself, your strengths, successes, gray areas, and weaknesses, and the ways you have limited yourself. This is a big part of what gives a Mastermind group its value. The facilitator must insist on this point so that participants learn to identify their challenges and weaknesses and transform them into opportunities for growth.

It is important to realize that being on the hot seat isn't necessarily an easy, comfortable experience... You will get a lot of different types of input, and that can upset you inside. It is at times a confrontational experience. The group, caring but not complacent, will push Johnny to his own limits, confront him with his contradictions and fears, and even sometimes about his lack of courage... It is under such conditions that Johnny's progress will be rapid and decisive. It is possible such an inter-action will unleash some waves of emotion in her/him. The freeing of blocked emotions is part of the process of human progress. These kinds of emotions can turn into true resources if they are understood and support-ed by others who are significant to us. Therefore, it is important that the entire group welcomes each other's emotions in a tactful, thoughtful way.

These emotions, which come into awareness and are then used intelli-gently can accelerate our professional achievements. Our emotions serve as levers that allow us to develop strong motivation; they guide us towards our goals, allow us to get beyond tense situations, reinforce our acuity for perceiving what is important in different situations, and help us master human relations better.

We have a vast repertoire of emotions. As of today, researchers are not in agreement about how many basic emotions there actually are. The main emotions, however, are joy, anger, sadness, and fear. Others that can be added to those are disgust and surprise, and more complex feelings like shame, pleasure, and love. There are a lot of other emotions, and the more the group members exercise the habit of acknowledging their own emotions, the more they will be able to recognize and respond to those of the others, since empathy comes about from self-awareness.

It is not uncommon for participants experience a number of these emotions when they are on the hot seat. The table on the following page gives some examples.

Emotions	Examples of emotions that might surface when one is on the hot seat:
Anger	* You feel angry with yourself because you become aware that you have, very unwisely, allowed opportunities that were obviously good and/or useful ones to pass by the wayside. * Certain participants tell you things that you think are false, or that you find annoying (even if they shared them with you out of caring). * You become aware that there is some obstacle that is keeping you from achieving your goal.
Joy	* You see a solution to a problem that has been blocking you for a long time. The situation becomes clear. * You reconsider a situation because of comments that others have formulated and change your point of view about it. That makes you feel joyful.
Fear	* You have known for a long time that you are going to have to do something that you have been putting off. You decide to take action, but you're still afraid.
Sadness	* You realize that you have lost important things because of a fear that you could have managed better. You notice your helplessness and you are overcome with a feeling of sadness.
Disgust	* A participant's proposed solution, or an idea that you have just had, disgusts you.
Surprise	* A participant seems to have understood things that you have been experiencing for a long time, or things that you have always kept hidden, whether you were aware of them or not.

There are a lot of other emotions. The more the participants learn to acknowledge their own emotions, the more they will be able to recognize those of others. And beyond just strengthening their emotional skills, participants will also develop social skills which will bolster their relationships with other people.

It is on the basis of these kinds of relationships that the Mastermind group establishes its unique effectiveness. The quality of the bonds and the feeling that one "belongs" allow a special "alliance" to develop between members. The group turns out to be excellent when the alliance is solid. It is there, to be exploited by everyone. It, without a doubt, creates a high level of energy within the group.

6.4 Taking Action

It is essential to keep in mind that it is through taking action that the application of knowledge and deep and long-lasting changes become concrete. That's why it's important that the Mastermind processes lead to concrete decisions about actions and not to vague hopes.

One of the most important of these processes consists of prompting participants to set up goals and then supporting them to take action so that each person achieves or exceeds her/his goals, modifies her/his professional activities, and takes advantage of the wealth of support that comes from the group. This creates an accelerator for success.

Therefore, the facilitator needs to be careful not to allow too much time for futile discussions that do not lead to action. On the other hand, personal exchanges have an important place in producing good group dynamics. So the facilitator needs to also respect the time that is set aside purely social exchanges at the beginning and end of the sessions.

For a project to be successful, it is necessary to come up with the basic idea, imagine all kinds of possibilities, look in a forward direction, define a vision and a strategy, consolidate everything, come up with solution, and above all, take action. Some Mastermind group participants have to make the decision that they will take a risk by taking action. There can be no procrastination of any kind if one is going to make quick progress.

A clear definition of goals and the criteria for success allows us to know if we are advancing toward out desired states. Each member of the group defines her/his goals, intentions and ambitions at the time of meetings and shares them with her/his peers. Each person allows herself/himself to say that she/he has the right to succeed with the project and to derive significant benefits from it. It is what is called the "big hairy audacious goal". We all have the right to be successful and to benefit a great deal from our efforts.

The facilitator supports each participant in the monitoring of her/his progress and by helping her/him succeed with her/his project. Like Alain Cardon says: *"Being able to decide only has meaning if one is able to monitor, over time, the implementation of her/his decisions. A law has no meaning without an application decree that includes specific information that has to do with applications and monitoring. It has to do with implementation measures that are put in place over a certain period of time. It is a matter of knowing how to measure one's progress during the carrying out of a project, a trip, or some trivial task, or during the carrying out of a complex mission that takes place over a period of years."* At every Mastermind group encounter, each participant explains what she/he has implemented, and where she/he is along the path to the realization of her/his goal's.

Let's return for a moment to the idea that emotions act as the trigger for taking action. Bringing emotions to life is one of the primary intentions of Mastermind methodology.

During the hot seat procedure, there is, for Johnny and his peers, several exchanges during which each participant's feelings are expressed. Therefore, every person learns to verbalize the emotions she/he experiences during the process. That isn't something that is necessarily all that habitual on the part of the participants. It does, however, represent a stepping stone that helps lead one into the future. Thus, it is necessary to learn to identify the emotions that run through us so we can develop better self-awareness and strengthen our perceptions of other people's emotions.

This type of empathetic feedback is fundamentally different from the rational kind of feedback that we more typically put into practice. Rational feedback, however, only triggers just a small bit of motivation. When Johnny receives feedback that is more intellectual and rational, he will, without a doubt, say to himself, "Yes, that's right. It would be good for me to think about studying the pertinence of what has been said to me. But I'll look into it later."

On the other hand, if Johnny is affected in the deepest part of his soul by a sincere, true and proper emotion that is meaningful to him, he will more likely say to himself, "Whoa!" They have figured it out correctly—that's really what I must do. Why didn't I realize it earlier? I really want to do what they mentioned or proposed. I feel like it will work. I'm going to work towards that, because I know that it will bring me what I want." That is indeed the kind of emotion that triggers decisive motivation. That is the kind of motivation that the facilitator wants to mobilize.

A Mastermind group is definitely one of the most effective ways, for any entrepreneurial person, to go beyond her/his limits and speed up her/his personal and professional success. Through this innovative approach, every member receives encouragement, ideas, advice, support, constructive challenges, and guidance... All of that will come about from the very specific, productive dynamics that are created by the group itself.

6.5 A Stimulating, Protective Framework, Inside of Which a Mastermind Group Functions

As with all group or team work, the framework established for the group's interaction should be adapted according to what the group's stated goals are. It is based on rules that allow certain things, and which prohibit certain other things. Together, the rules regulate all of the group's interaction to its benefit.

A Mastermind group brings together people who have common goals, which almost always have to do with entrepreneurship and business leadership. Group members learn together and cultivate "collective intelligence" because of the different Mastermind group processes, especially the hot seat. These processes provide structure to the group's exchanges, and support participants to take action. But the pertinence and effectiveness of a peer group is linked to the values, principles and rules that all of the members must share and respect. That is how its success is ensured. The facilitator must make the rules for the group's functioning explicit, so that the group, and the self-regulation that takes place inside of it, will function effectively.

Group work can amount to the best or worst of things. The best thing is that it is stimulating, a source of individual and collective reflection, and becomes even more effective as it promotes the taking of action. The worst thing about it is that time can be wasted on chit-chat, even on unproductive conflicts, to the detriment of making of decisions and taking action.

It is necessary, however, to avoid imposing too many rules. They might lose their effectiveness just because there's so many of them, so that participants might forget about them and no longer respect them. It seems to us sufficient to define a few principles that support the functioning and harmony of the group, the emergence of generative collaborations and the desire to stretch oneself. These founding principles need to be broad enough so that they can be adapted to different situations, and sufficiently clear so that each participant is aware of what she/he can do, and what she/he shouldn't do.

The facilitator will, of course, present these principles, which support the smooth functioning of the group, and submit them to the members of the group at the time of its creation. In that case, all members are actually practicing the principle of co-responsibility. Mastermind groups will be able to evolve the principles, as well as the rules for implementing them, depending on how mature they are, and what their needs are.

The facilitator will need to spend a sufficient amount of time when launching her/his Mastermind group to present and explain its principles of functioning and the values the represent, so that each person understands how the principles support the group's functioning and the growth of the members. A shrewd facilitator will have participants sign an internal policy document so that the group members' commitment is clear, and so that she/he will be able to refer to it, if need be. In particular, if it turns out to be necessary to exclude a member from a group, the facilitator will want to be able to rely on those commitments.

The enlistment of new members has already been addressed, to a large extent, in previous chapters. Let's just recall, from what was stated before, that it is essential for the group's goals to be clear, transparent, and accepted by each new member before she/he joins, in particular when it comes to her/his agreeing to these founding principles.

In addition to bringing in new participants, there is also the issue of asking someone to leave, if necessary. In particular, there is the question of how to exclude an individual who causes dysfunction in the group, or who doesn't respect the rules; or even understand how to do that.

Facilitators who are just starting out might be afraid to oust a member from their Mastermind group. Asking a participant to leave the group might, however, might be a necessary decision when it's a question of saving the group. The other group members might blame the facilitator, question her/his professionalism, and may even look at her/him as a coward, if she/he decides to allow a member who is not respecting the rules and principles of the group to stay.

Ousting a member from the group will make some participants happy; but it can also create a stir among others, when the person in question has gotten along well with them. Because of that, they will not understand why she/he has to be excluded. The facilitator will need to explain, in a clear and honest way, the reasons for her/her decision and to rely solely on facts. It is quite obvious that the facilitator will want bring up the issue with the member in question in private first, and will listen to what she/he has to say. The facilitator can consult with the rest of the Mastermindians; but in the end, the decision is up to her/him. If it is a Mastermind group where one has to pay, the facilitator will have an interest in specifying, in her/his contract, if any ousted members will or will not be entitled to any reimbursement.

These rules are set up so that there can be a structure that protects each group member. It supports each member to express herself/himself freely and authentically, out of respect for her/her as an individual, and for the entire group of members. The rules also allow the facilitator to take control of difficult situations, such as member procrastination, absenteeism, or disruptive behavior.

1 – Principle of Regular ATTENDANCE and PUNCTUALITY

The success of Mastermind groups depends on how long they actually stay in existence. All participants are required to attend every meeting. Therefore, each of them has to personally commit to that. The meetings are always planned in advance, anyway. Mastermindians should not allow phone calls, e-mails, or side conversations to disrupt what goes on in sessions.

Upon her/his arrival in the group, each member agrees to commit to it for the period that has been defined by its creator. Mastermind group are necessarily "long-lasting" in order to support the type of changes that participants will be capable of making while the group is going on.

Groups usually go on for a year; but that can vary, depending on the group. Some group leaders offer trial periods, at the end of which the new arrivals commit to attending for one year.

At the end of this period, any participant can leave the Mastermind group or continue her/his participation in it, as long as she/he follows the rules that have been established. It is best if those who want to leave a Mastermind group let their decision be known one or two months in advance. That allows those involved to have enough time to respectfully wrap up any ongoing collaborations, which will likely have been powerful and emotional. It also allows the group to celebrate, in a way that is special, the departing members' successes at the time of their departure.

Anyone who is absent from the group has to let everybody know why she/he couldn't attend. In the event of an absence, the money for the meeting is still due. This rule is in place to make sure that group's framework remains strong, and to facilitate inclusion and commitment.

Each person commits to showing up just prior to the start of in-person or virtual meetings, out of respect for the group.

Punctuality and regular attendance are two key indicators of each person's level of commitment towards the group, her/his own goals, and her/his capacity for stretching herself/himself. The group's synergy and dynamics can be negatively affected even if just one of the members holds the others back by not respecting these basic rules.

2 – Principle of CO-RESPONSIBILITY and COMMITMENT

Peer groups often function by using the principle of co-responsiblity as their foundation. This principle is aimed at having each person in the group think of herself/himself as responsible for the success of the other members, as well as for her/his own success. Each individual works for the achievement of her/his own goals, as well as those of her/his peers. Each individual is also responsible for making sure that the meetings develop in a good way; that is to say, she/he should participate in a way that contributes to good group dynamics, by having the right attitude, and through her/his involvement.

To promote the effectiveness of the group sessions, each person prepares for upcoming meetings incorporating any feedback that followed from previous meetings. This may include the times that she/he will be on the hot seat, or if she/he has important information to communicate, or to any other requests she/he might make for support.

One of the key expectations for each individual in the Mastermind group is that she/he will take action. Every participant is responsible for the commitments that she/he decides to make as part of the group. She/He only announces what actions she/he is going to take if she/he thinks that she/he will be able to keep her/his commitments, or is at least able to mobilize some resources to try to achieve them. If the participant is unable to successfully carry out those commitments, she/he informs others about it and points to it as being an experience from which she/he learned. That makes it easier for her/him to then move in the right direction.

To quote Ed Catmull, President of Pixar: "Mistakes aren't a necessary evil. They are no evil at all. They are the inevitable consequence when anyone has to deal with anything new... They should be thought of as valuable."[2]

Every participant commits to implementing the necessary steps to achieve her/his goals, which should always be ambitious ones. Each individual is the judge of what is good for her/him, and of what decisions she/he should make. And each participant assumes entire responsibility for taking or not taking action. Mastermindians should therefore be focused on the goals to be achieved and on making a very high level of commitment in relation to themselves and their group. Each participant allows herself/himself to be confronted by her/his difficulties, weaknesses, gray areas, and fears, so she/he can get beyond them.

---

2   *Harvard Business Review*, December 2016-January 2017, No. 18, Birkinshaw, Julian, and Haas, Martine. *Learn from Your Failures – Increase the Returns from Your Failures*, p. 44.

From that point on, each Mastermindian becomes a "partner in responsibility" with all of the other members.

This has to do with the reciprocal commitment that we talked about earlier. Each person acts to serve herself/himself and also serves the other participants. Everyone invests her/his efforts in what goes on in the group; each person agrees to be open with the other participants, based on her/his own experience and knowledge, so she/he can help them progress. Each member agrees to contribute her/his help and support, and to receive help from other participants.

It is also important that each participant's commitment be fully active during group encounters; everyone is focused on what is going on. Each member should be available for each individual who expresses herself/himself, by listening to her/him, and by being of service. She/He should be totally focused on what she/he thinks is most useful for the other person. Starting group encounters with the COACH state, as was explained previously in this book, helps to more rapidly create optimal conditions for group interactions.

3 – Principle of TRUST

Trust cannot be taken for granted. It emerges naturally when a group of conditions that promote it are met.

Each group member needs to embrace the principle that trust between participants is necessary for each one of them to have greater success, and for collective dynamics to work. Participants commit to trusting the others during the organized activities that the facilitator sets up.

Patrick Lencioni, an American lecturer and author of several books, explains that trust is the certainty that each member of a group has that their peers' intentions are good, and that it is unnecessary to be on one's guard, since her/his vulnerability will not be used against her/him.

Trust is brought to life in a group through actions, gestures, words, and the caring attention that the members pay to one another. It is based on shared experiences which are associated with strong emotions. Trust emerges—it either appears or it doesn't. All the facilitator can do is create an environment in which participants are going to feel comfortable enough with one another, so that trust can grow.

The members of a group in which there is no trust do not allow themselves to engage, and do not acknowledge their weaknesses and doubts, so they can move beyond them; neither do they share the mistakes they have made with others so that they can be turned into learning experiences.

On the other hand, when the members of a group feel like they trust one another, they don't try to protect themselves, as if they're wearing armor. They can invest their time and energy in their relationships, and in the service of their project and their own growth, and not in defense or attack strategies, nor in futile psychological games. Since they feel serene, they take the risk of undertaking more initiatives, and spontaneously offer their help.

Depending on their history, education, career path, and personality, some people are able to be trusting more quickly, while others need a period of getting used to the others.

Every participant should, at the minimum, recognize that trust between members is necessary for each of them to have a higher degree of success, and so that collective "magic" can work. As you will notice if you participate in a Mastermind group, it is not so easy to engage with people whom you do not know. To make progress, whether financially or as a human being, one has to overcome a certain amount of modesty, confront herself/himself, lay herself/himself bare, and be aware of her/his limitations so she/he can get beyond them more easily. Talking about oneself is an easy, pleasant exercise for some participants, while for others it can be difficult and trying. It's the same when it comes to exposing one's projects if trust has not yet emerged. People will be afraid that the other participants steal her/his ideas This fear never exists in a group where trust has been established.

The facilitator, therefore, has an important role when it comes to the emergence of trust. Does she/he formulate a clear, secure framework? Do the rules that she/he proposes give the participants the desire to be engaged? Does she/he take the time to build a quality relationship with each participant? Does she/he give a powerful demonstration of the great principle of caring, and even more than that, caring without complacency?

Nowadays, it cannot be denied that, even inside of a global context and with the exponential growth of information, each one of us still only has part of the knowledge and skills that are needed for our work. Therefore, it is essential for us to strengthen our network and to rely on other people who fill in gaps in our expertise and professional knowledge, and to do so with complete confidence.

Therefore, the facilitator will need to pay particular attention to creating an overall context that will promote trust and sharing; factors which are essential for the effectiveness of a Mastermind group.

4 – Principle of HONESTY and CARING

One of the things that a Master-mind promises to do is to allow every participant to make rapid progress, whether it relates to her/his professional activity or to her/his personal development. And we don't believe that can be accomplished by avoiding the mention of the weak points that we perceive in others, or in their work, since we want to help everyone quickly. As partners in responsibility, the participants should, therefore, offer one another honest, sincere feedback that will help unleash some quantum leaps. A Mastermind

"You know you can tell us how you feel".

group is a space where lightning fast experimentation and learning takes place. Participants' feedback should also be lightning fast.

Participants also apply this principle of honesty and caring without complacency— being caring at the same time that one is demanding—to the facilitator.

The Mastermindians should tell her/him what they want and need; like how they would like to see the group's content and the processes evolve. The facilitator should be open to listening to those kinds of remarks, which are, of course, constructive as long as she/he has adopted the principle of caring without complacency herself/himself.

This rule allows for an environment where nothing goes unspoken and cliques can be avoided. It favors inclusion and promotes the re-integration of energy, which is of use to everyone.

The facilitator must be careful not to try to control the group; just like she/he should make sure that no other person be allowed to take control of it. There can be strong personalities that always want to get the upper hand over the others from the very first moment they join a group. Such dominating personalities should be allowed to express themselves but should not be allowed to disturb the emergence of the group's dynamics, which are necessary in this case. Likewise, the facilitator should allow for a large margin of freedom for the participants, at the same time that she/he maintains the structure of the process, so that planned group processes can easily take place.

Caring should be a reigning principle among participants. This caring is expressed through respectful words and actions, as well as by a desire to help others. Caring, as a principle, is caring that is unconditional, and is offered freely, without knowing the other. One offers it to fellow participants for the simple and good reason that she/he is part of the same Mastermind group and that she/he is a human being.

The group is a place of experimentation and learning for each participant. Each person has the right to "not know" before becoming aware, and to "not understand" before she/he ends up understanding.

Caring, however, does not always mean that one has to use kid gloves with other participants. A frank kind of honesty should also exist between the participants. That implies that difficult things can be said, if that will indeed cause a participant to make progress, and if, in particular, there are differences between what she/he says and reality. It is not a matter of protecting the others, but of helping them grow.

Caring without complacency, or caring by making demands, are factors that lead to success for a Mastermind group. The members need to carry out constructive criticism and to distance themselves from prejudices and useless, overly kind remarks that one might make so that the person on the receiving end won't feel upset.

All feedback should be oriented towards the improvement of the other and her/his professional activity and should contain some openings towards solutions. It should be a source of useful information. Feedback should not consist of any kind of value judgment, or of any terse, judgmental remarks, such as "you are wrong," or "that really isn't a problem".

Feedback (or the returning of comments, as a response to another member's comments) should not contain anything that could be interpreted as a personal attack, or as making fun of the person who is receiving it. These kinds of communication blunders might make the receiver feel inhibited, and will prevent her/him from hearing or identifying suggestions for her/his improvement. Even worse, she/he might stage a counter-attack. By contrast, every option that is future-oriented develops participants' potential.

Psychoanalyst Harry Levinson proposes that the following four elements be applied to feedback, so that it will be a source of improvement:

* Be precise and specific.
* Offer suggestions and open up new possibilities that have not been identified by the person in question.
* Be present for the other so that personalized communication can be established.

* Be sensitive, that is, aware of the impact that your words might have on the person, and show empathy for her/him.

Here is an excerpt about a situation that took place during one of our Mastermind groups. It illustrates the principle of caring without complacency:

Nice, January 2016. A participant goes on the hot seat and brings up an economic challenge that is part of a real estate development project. He wants feedback from other Mastermindians. At the end of his presentation, after a phase when impressions are shared, and after questions, so that his situation can be clarified, the other participants offer their feedback to Johnny. Most of them contribute ideas, proposals, and more than anything else, support, because it seems that something is not totally developed, that Johnny is hesitating and doesn't know where to start. However, one of the Mastermindians is going to do the exact opposite of what the others are doing; he will not contribute any ideas or encouragement. On the contrary, he is going to challenge Johnny and his project by telling him that he doesn't believe in it, and that he has the impression that Johnny is bringing in somebody else's project, and since that is what he is doing, he will have a hard time bringing it to a successful conclusion.

One needs to understand that the support that is thrown into the mix by those initial Mastermindians, and the confrontation carried out by the last one, are both at the same level of caring. The caring that is present in a Mastermind group also consists of promoting Johnny's progress by allowing him to confront his own limitations and get beyond them. If it is necessary to destabilize him so he can better succeed, then there is no reason for the last participant to refrain from that action. The participant who will not intervene because she/he thinks that her/his opinion might upset Johnny isn't carrying out her/his role as partner in responsibility the way she/he should.

The confrontation directed at Johnny is a gift that is given to him, in the same way that all the really great ideas are, as long as it allows Johnny to grow, broaden his scope and perspectives on solutions, develop his leadership, and strengthen his business model.

Therefore, the principle of caring in a Mastermind group is a bit different from the one that is usually present in training, development, or co-development groups. Most of the time, being caring in a group consists of expressing things in a way that is very measured so that the person who is receiving the feedback will never be shocked or upset, by words, or because of expressed attitudes. In a Mastermind group, caring amounts to a general principle of caring rather than to any specific form of caring. Showing complacency in relation to others does not help them advance in their goals. We therefore think that the idea that there should be caring without complacency should be prominent in a Mastermind group; that is to say, caring should be coupled with some form of demand for action in relation to the other.

That is what a great part of the specific power of Mastermind groups consists of; and it is what visionary business leaders show up to look for.

A Mastermind group can obviously decide to function based on principles of caring that are more "typical", such as those that are used for co-development groups.

We first of all advise the facilitator to ask Johnny, before each time that he goes on the hot seat, if he wants to be handled with kid gloves (principle of typical caring) or if he is amenable to being destabilized a bit (principle of demanding caring, that is to say, without any complacency).

Beyond caring without complacency, there can be friction within the group. That is not serious in and of itself. The question there is whether or not the group will enter what we have called a CRASH state, which can be counter-productive; though even CRASH states, if properly managed, can introduce new resources. And anyway, all great relationships need productive confrontations.

Healthy confrontation can be productive in the sense that it allows participants to delve deeply into an issue, instead of forever putting it off. It allows them to debate with passion, based on their own ideas. On the other hand, the facilitator should quickly handle personality conflicts, since there is a risk that they could be harmful for the entire group.

5 – Principle of CONFIDENTIALITY and APPROPRIATENESS OF IDEAS

Confidentiality is, of course, THE key factor when it comes to any group of peers. It's a hallowed principle that the facilitator should regularly remind the participants of.

Therefore, each Mastermindian agrees that she/he will never divulge, at any time, now or in the future, what has been said in her/his group, nor anything about the situations and feelings that were shared between members. What is said inside of the group belongs to the group and no one else. Any infraction of this rule might turn out to be a valid reason to ask the instigator to leave the group, even though those kinds of indiscretions are, more often than not, involuntary, and rarely intentional.

If this situation does come about, a discussion should take place, preferably inside of the group, so that a collective decision can be made about what is going to be done. Every group will have an interest in determining what can and cannot be said about such a situation. For example, is it wrong to divulge the name of the people who make up a Mastermind group? On this point, we think that one should be able to say who is a part of our group. A Mastermind group is not some kind of secret clique but a group that carries out reciprocal development.

Confidentiality is something that has to do with the appropriateness of ideas that are presented. Although the ideas that emerge from the group do not belong to just one single person, those that an individual participant contributes do belong to her/him. Each participant, obviously, has to abstain from using, to her/his advantage, an idea or project that has been shared by another member.

Some collaborations on those ideas and projects could, of course, come about and become established inside of a Mastermind group. In effect, the participants, generally speaking, complement one another, since the facilitator always follows the principle to select people involved in different types of activities. The risk of there being competition among the members is, because of that, usually small, especially if the facilitator has done a good job of recruitment for her/his group from the start. This ensures that the conditions are in place for participants to find business opportunities that they can carry out together.

Emulation by one Mastermindian of another or other Mastermindians is an important phenomenon, but it should not lead to a climate of competition. If that does occur, the facilitator will need to take all necessary measures that will put an end to that kind of situation. A conflict of this type within the group, if not ironed out, can have a very negative affect on the group dynamics.

6 – *Principle of PLEASURE and CONVIVIALITY*

We have saved the most important principle for last. The sessions are supposed to be pleasant and convivial at the same time that they are venues for work and development. Each participant agrees that she /he will maintain a curious, open frame of mind towards the other members of the group, so that a true connection is established between group members.

Establishing bonds with the other group members, taking an interest in their issues, sharing, and exchanging banter are the main driving force behind the process of building a group. the dynamics of a Mastermind sessions should be one that brings participants pleasure.

High quality interaction takes place when we try out iconic venues that have character, or choose spots that the participants find inspiring, while they, at the same time, don't allow their egos to get carried away.

And above all, let's remember that we learn, become innovative, and get moving on things when the space we inhabit brings pleasure, a chance for emulation, and trust.

The Toltec Agreements, by Don Miguel Ruiz[3]

In addition to the principles we have presented, we think it is also important to include the 5 Toltec agreements that the Mexican writer, Miguel Ruiz, made popular. These "logical" qualities have relevance in all human relationships. The Mastermind group is no exception.

1. **Be impeccable with your words.** Speak with integrity. Say only what you mean. Avoid using your words to speak against yourself or to gossip about others. Use the power of your words in the support of truth and love.

2. **No matter what happens, don't take anything personally.** What others say and do is nothing more than a projection of their own reality, of their own map of the world. When you are immune to that, you are no longer the victim of useless suffering.

3. **Don't make assumptions.** Have the courage to ask questions and express your true desires. Communicate clearly with others to avoid sadness, misunderstandings, and drama. This agreement, on its own, has the power to change your life completely.

4. **Always do your best.** Your "best" changes from moment to moment, no matter what the circumstances. Simply do your best so that you can avoid blaming and judging yourself, and so that you won't have any regrets.

5. **Be skeptical, but learn to listen.** Don't believe yourself or anybody else. Use the power of doubt to question everything you hear: Is it really the truth? Listen for the intention behind the words; you will then understand the real message.

---

3   Ruiz, M. Les quatre accords Toltèques, 2016, Éditions Jouvence.

Conclusion

Santa Cruz, California
August 2016

So now it's over. 10 days of training in collective intelligence, with 40 people of 26 different nationalities, in the heart of California. 10 days of integrating the tools of generative collaboration, of course, but above all, 10 days when 40 people began to dream together about the world of tomorrow: about conscious leadership, caring organizations, or even next generation neighborhoods between individuals in the future. Each group reflected on its vision, mission, and ambition with regard to its project. It was a beautiful thing to see all the energy, enthusiasm, and things that resonated among the participants, who were in touch with their deep desire.

At the moment when each group was asked to go from the dream to the realization of the project, that is to say, to identify what each person needed to get to the point that she/he could continue the momentum, once she/he got back home, the need for a support group seemed obvious to me. Each person was going to go back to her/his country, alone, and take with her/him a wonderful kind of hope. But I was unable to stop myself from being afraid that it would quickly fade once she/he had to take up her/his usual daily activities again; even though not all dreams, of course, are called upon to become reality. What if Mastermind groups could become part of these spaces of transition between what is inside of us and all of the possibilities on the outside? Could it be that a well-meaning kick in the behind would compel us to keep our aspirations going and give them concrete form?

As I write this, I am thinking about the video that is going around on the Internet right now. It shows a small Asian boy who is participating in a gymnastic presentation. One sees him as he tries to jump over his vaulting obstacle. Dressed in his regulation gear, he tries to do it once, twice, three times, and each time, the obstacle is just too high. One can read the discouragement on his face. All of a sudden, all the other kids run up to him, on the instructions of their coach. Arm in arm, they surround him, encouraging him. The volume of their high-pitched voices, which blend together to throw support behind him, goes up. As they go back to their places, it is easy to see that the boy's confidence is renewed. He makes his next attempt with a new kind of energy, triumphantly leaping over the obstacle, well above the level of his previous attempts. All of the spectators are jubilant.

Isn't that like what we have been talking about since the beginning of this book?

Similar to what happened in the example of this young athlete, the Mastermind group offers you support that will vastly improve your performance. Like him, you are trying to surmount your own obstacles in relation to your personal and professional life and you are aware of the need to receive help to get there. You want help that will force you to get beyond your limitations, not just gradually, but rather in way that is lightning-fast, in the form of a major breakthrough.

You should be aware that it's not up to others to get you over your obstacles; that implies that they are going to do it for you. But the quality of the bond between the members of the groups, and the caring without complacency that takes place among participants, associated with a structured process, are both elements that will make you feel highly supported in an environment of trust.

Your whole being is called upon—what you're thinking, your emotions, and your body tunes in to the group's frequency. The group becomes engaged with you and works for you. It reflects a collective harmony. It is the kind of harmony that is far removed from co-dependence and group thinking. Instead, it is harmony that is based upon the recognition of and the synergy that is found between differences.

Of course, the most important thing, in the end, is what actually takes place in Mastermind groups. Even though it is a key part of the process, going on the hot seat is not enough to ensure success if you don't take action between meetings. Because, deep down, that is where the real competition is: within yourself, in action. But again the group is with you. Urging you on and at the same time they are giving you their full support.

The facilitator guarantees that the group's framework is flexible enough but at the same time provides sufficient structure. She/He is the one who orchestrates the group's collective chemistry. She/He is its guardian. She/He is responsible for the selection of participants, based on their diversity and the wealth of ideas and experiences that they offer. The facilitator also selects the processes of collective intelligence for the group, so that it will be greater than the sum of its parts. She/He, in short, is as much a caring organizer as she/he is a master of ceremonies and a keeper of time; a combination of an iron fist and a velvet glove. For a Mastermind group to succeed, nothing can be left to chance. At the same time, a great deal of room must be devoted to promote a generative spirit and to support what emerges from the group's interactions.

And then, if all of these elements gel together, you might just experience a space where the goal is not just success but one of self-realization; a place where action is tied in with meaning, where engagement turns into discipline, where the task to be accomplished is developed through the pleasure and the richness of relationships. All of this gives the ego the chance to give up its preeminent place in favor of a project that is greater than itself, thanks to the other participants.

A final comment: This book was inspired by several interviews with facilitators and participants in Mastermind groups, some of whom are international renowned. The answer to the question, "What is the best advice you can give to someone who wants to put together her/his own group?" is one that is unanimous: "If you want to come up with a quality Mastermind group, you should become a participant in a Mastermind group yourself. Your experience as a participant will solidify your convictions about its effectiveness, which is something that is necessary, so that you can make decisions in relation to those who might be participants in your own group in the future. The fact that you have made the effort to develop yourself will speak volumes on your behalf."

Checklist for the Creation of a Mastermind Group

* What kind of Mastermind group do you want to create?

* What will be its purpose?

* What values will it espouse?

* What will it be called?

* How large will your group be?

* How much will it cost?

* What personal qualities do you have so that support you to facilitate this group?

* What skills do you have that will allow you to be the leader/ facilitator of a Mastermind group?

* What skills, competencies, and experiences will you bring to the group?

* What skills are you lacking?

* What kind of processes will you use during the Mastermind group sessions?

* How demanding are you going to be when it comes to participants making a commitment to take action?

* What aspects of the group's framework will be co-constructed, and which will be non-negotiable?

* What kind of profiles are more in tune with your vision for your Mastermind group?

* Who is your Number One choice for your group? Why?

* Who would be your Number Two, three, Four, Five, Six, Seven? Why?

* How often will your sessions take place?

* On what date(s) will your sessions take place?

* How long will they last?

* What procedure are you going to use so you can keep to the group schedule, as you have planned it, and so that the timing associated with it will be respected?

* Where will your Mastermind group be held?

* How will participants be supported so they can prepare for sessions?

* How will the participants be supported so they can stay in contact between sessions?

* How will the participants be supported so they can make a commitment to the group?

* How are you going to create the group's title?

* How are you going to create trust among the members of the group?

* How are you going to recruit members?

* What will you do when you need to exclude members from your group?

* How are you going to evaluate the progress of your group's members? (When are you going to do that?)

To support you when you attempt to answer all of these questions later on, the authors of this book are in a position to offer you training so you can create and lead a Mastermind group.

About the Co-Authors

Eric BAUDET spent more than 30 years in the management and training business and found that he had a passion for the mechanisms that drive team dynamics, leadership, and collective intelligence.

He has been certified, by Dilts Strategy Group, as a facilitator and trainer in collective intelligence. He is active in different research groups and deploys collective intelligence in organizations, through training, support, conferences, workshops, and Mastermind groups.

His vision is that of seeing systems elevated to a higher level of awareness and performance, so that each player can calmly discover her/his way and thrive. To know more about him go to: http://eb-consult.fr

Céline BAYSELLIER is a certified executive business coach and facilitator of workplace relations. An associate at Institut Adelante, she leads/organizes interventions by relying on tools of collective intelligence collaboration, creativity, emulation, and the taking of responsibility. She holds an advanced degree in Human Resources, is a Neuro-Linguistic Programming coach, and is certified in team and personal coaching. She was trained in collective intelligence and leadership training, while a member of a group led by Robert Dilts, and now fully practices the Mastermind group process, like the seven other authors of this book. Member of vision 2021 network.

Olivier CHRISTOL is a certified executive business coach and a trainer who has been trained in collective intelligence by the Dilts Strategy Group. After more than 20 years as an engineer and manager for international business groups, he now supports businesses by helping them develop the engagement of collaborators, optimize the performance of teams, develop skills, free energies, make a common vision emerge, get projects of transformation going, and bring innovations to life. Passionate about collective intelligence, he facilitates Mastermind groups for entrepreneurs and managers of micro-, small, and medium-sized enterprises.

Christophe GENRE-JEZELET is General Services Director for the Commune known as Bouches-du-Rhône. Trained in both personal and collective coaching, as well as in mediation, his interests lie in individual and team effectiveness. He intervenes, using the theme of the development of collective intelligence, at different institutes (CNFPT, Sciences Po…) and facilitates professional and human resources development. He is one of the founding members of the Vision 2021 Association, the social agenda of which is to spread the principles of collective intelligence to organizations, and throughout society. He is author of a book about positive thinking, "Et si je prenais la vie du bon côté!", which has been published by Édition Eyrolles. He offers conferences on the theme of positive thinking, so that one can have better health, and develop a better relationship with herself/himself and society.

Nadia GRANDCLEMENT's motto: "It's not about what you do, it's about how you do it" She is certified executive business Coach, NLP Master Practitioner, certified as a group facilitator in collective intelligence by the Dilts Strategy Group, and trainer in the fields of management, communication, and sales. After several years of experience in International companies , she helps organizations in their transformation. She thinks that all of us can create a more respectful world together, where each individual will be able to express her/his talents. To find out more, go to: www.Calliope-consulting.fr.
Member of vision 2021 network

Catherine PENA is a systemic coach, facilitator in collective intelligence and a teacher in economics and management in Aix-Marseille University. After more than 10 years of experience in the management of companies, she helps organizations, their managers and teams to re-awaken their potential, improve their well-being and optimize their resources together to achieve lasting results Which sometimes exceed the initial targets. Leadership, reciprocity and pleasure guide its field interventions. A member of several research and experimentation groups on leadership and Mastermind, she is involved in the development of collective intelligence within the Dilts / Vision 2021 network

Laurent DE RAUGLAUDRE is always on the hunt to find a good way to define himself... He likes to lead marches through the desert, and to write and offer advice about management and responsibility (http://je-suis-manager.com/). He has accumulated a wealth of experience, when it comes to international management, in a highly successful high tech company that has seen strong growth, then as a business adviser to specific individuals. His training in collective intelligence has helped him develop his strong belief that every individual is a storehouse of a great many treasures that should be shared with others, and that the issue at hand often surfaces as a result of the their discovery...

Jean François THIRIET is a trainer and facilitator of collective intelligence certified by the Dilts Strategy Group. Thanks to his experience of the Mastermind groups as a facilitator and participant, he wishes both to professionalize and to put at the disposal of all these powerful accelerators of success and the collective intelligence. Author of "J'ai décidé d'être heureux au travail", "Se préparer à résoudre un conflit," and "Pratique de la gratitude". You can find out more about him at: www.jftformation.fr. - Member of vision 2021 network

Bibliography

* Goleman, D., *L'intelligence émotionnelle,* 2014, J'ai Lu.

* Cardon, A., *Coaching d'équipe,* 2014, Eyrolles.

* Deering, A., Russel, J. and Dilts, R., *Alpha Leadership, les 3 A: anticiper, aligner, agir,* 2009, De boeck.

* De Saint Exupéry, A., *Le Petit Prince,* Paris 1943, Gallimard

* Dilts, R,. and DeLozier, J., Bacon Dilts, D., *NLP II: The Next Generation*, Meta Publications, Capitola, 2010.

* Dilts, R., *Next Generation Entrepreneurs*, Dilts Strategy Group, Santa Cruz 2015

* Dilts, R., *Generative Collaboration*, Dilts Strategy Group, Santa Cruz 2016

* Dilts, R., *Conscious Leadership and Resilience*, Dilts Strategy Group, Santa Cruz 2017

* Eskenazi, S., *Les règles d'une supervision collective.*

* Lencioni, P., *Optimisez votre équipe,* 2006, Un monde différent.

* Payette, A., and Champagne, C., 2002, *Le groupe de Codéveloppement professionnel,* Presse de l'Université du Québec.

* Surowiecki, J., *La sagesse des foules*, 2008, Jean-Claude Lattes Édition.

Useful Links

We thank all of those who have agreed to share their wealth of experience with Mastermind groups with us. Here are their websites:

* Alex Barker: Alexbarker.co

* Yvonne Gerard: https://www.createmyindependence.com

* Karyn Greenstreet: http://www.TheSuccessAlliance.com

* Nick LaForce: http://www.nickleforce.com/

* Xavier Lee: http://corelc.org/your-core-leaders

* Colette Normandeau: http://www.colettenormandeau.com

* Dorothy A. Martin-Neville: www.askdrdorothy.com

* Laurie Wann: www.intentionalentrepreneurs.com

Useful Resources on the Web

* *http://www.metasysteme-coaching.fr/francais/introduc-tion-aux-micro-competences-systemiques/*

* *http://www.marcdussault.com/how-to-create-a-mastermind-group*

* *http://jonathanmilligan.com/how-to-launch-a-mastermind-group/*

* *http://www.jayfiset.com/tag/mastermind/*

* *http://www.metasysteme-coaching.fr/francais/introduc-tion-aux-micro-competences-systemiques/*

* *Vision 2021: www.vision-2021.fr*

* *Formation Évolution et Synergie: http://www.coaching-pnl.org/coaching-pnl/*

* *http://www.diltsstrategygroup.com*

* *http://www.robertdilts.com*

APPENDIX

Synthesis of the Collective Intelligence Mastermind Group Model

What will make your Mastermind group unique, original, and powerful?

Mastermind groups come in several forms; some even come about from direct marketing. The added value we are proposing, the difference that makes all the difference, is the contribution of collective intelligence, which will catalyze this already powerful process, in order to increase, tenfold, the generative effects and phenomena related to the emergence of ideas.

Our model can be summarized by seven key stages:

1 – The creation of a group field that is favorable for the emergence of a 3rd mind, the master mind

This is the essence of any Mastermind group. As Napoleon Hill pointed out, the "mastermind" emerges from interactions where 1 + 1 = 3, or more. Practices that support the development of a generative state (where group members are centered in themselves, focused on a common intention and connected to their resources) help group members to form this third mind more quickly and easily. These practices strengthen the group members' capacity for opening up—opening up the heart and leaving prejudices behind, and opening up the mind by putting aside judgments and assumption. Such a generative state allows group members to let go of limitations and to let new ideas come. a good example of this is regularly practicing the C.O.A.C.H. state until one can consistently recognize and reach an optimal mindset.

2 – Group inclusiveness and wind-up of meetings

Times for inclusion (i.e., getting input from each group member) are very important but often non-existent in group interactions. Ensuring that each member contributes is important for people to form connections so that they are in tune with one another and can play a beautiful symphony. Moments of inclusion put people in a state of resonance so that new ideas can emerge. One of the effects of inclusion is to put people on equal footing when it comes to speaking and to their importance to the group, whether they are introverts or extraverts. This is a subtle way of dealing with people who have strong personalities. It will lead to a feeling of psychological safety, which is necessary for the group dynamic to be successful. The regular inclusion of input from all group members also allows for the creation of strong relationships, trust and the opening of authentic dialogue. It is also important that, at the end of each meeting, there is a period of reflection and setting commitment to action before people leave.

3 – Take the time to share your intent

Intent is important for the collective intelligence process. How will I engage and what will I contribute during this meeting? Why am I here? What kind of presence will I have? One's intent is where passion and motivation to take action begin. It is the reason why we join the Mastermind group to begin with. It is essential to regularly share intention, starting with when the group first comes into existence, and then at every meeting that follows and to focus all you attention on it. It is even preferable for the facilitator to share her/his intent a few days before a meeting—its effect will only become intensified. Sharing one's intent is a process that becomes a part of the process of inclusion. The intention should be expressed in an uncomplicated way, in a few words, through a metaphor, image, impression, feeling, or emotion. Expressing an intention directs the level of energy and commitment, and the state of mind participants will be in during the Mastermind sessions.

4 – Take care to focus as much attention on the individual as on the group

In order to maintain good group dynamics, there has to be back and forth exchanges between the individual and the other members. That allows the group's richness, generated by individual differences and diversity, to be sustained. It is important to bear in mind that everything starts with the individual.

But it is also important to see to it that there is balance and alignment between individual participants and what goes on during the group. In particular, the time should be balanced out between talking, individual and group work, and the number of sessions on the hot seat...

There should be alignment between each individual participant and the group's purpose and the values it reflects. The quality of interaction that takes place also allows the development of individual and group support of the members, which will help develop the phenomena of engagement and co-responsibility.

That also allows for the development of a sense of unity and a feeling of psychological safety, which is the very essence of a Mastermind group.

5 – Use the three kinds of intelligence (cognitive, somatic and field) that are a part of collective intelligence processes

The emotional and cognitive intelligence of the field should be a part of all of the processes. The three kinds of intelligence that are used in all of the processes are a catalyst for one another; their effects are enhanced. That is one of the foundations of collective intelligence.

These three intelligences together are the basis for intuition. Someone who led a workshop at the time of one of our conferences contributed the following comment: "I am now going to go with my gut and let what happens happen!"

6 – Facilitate in such a way so that things take place more easily

The facilitator's ability to manage the Mastermind group process, such as the hot seat, is crucial to the success of the group. Her/His role consists of clearly and consistently guiding the group's processes. She/He will need to be able to use, to maximum advantage, the number of individuals who are present (with their diversity and differences), the group (the collective), and the interactions that take place (which increase with the number of participants) so that the mission of the group can be carried out. It should be noted that when 10 people get together, they create a field in which there are potentially 45 possible interactions at any time. Our experience coincides with the conclusion made by Google's "Project Aristotle", which asserts that "the quality of interactions is more important that the quality of each individual." Thus, it is important to focus a very particular kind of attention on group interactions, without overlooking each individual.

7 – Commitment

The emergence of ideas, as great as it is, is of no use if nothing is put into practice. It is necessary to make time in the different processes to focus on the issue of commitment. Difficulties with commitment can happen at any time, and in different ways. There can be difficulties in making a commitment at the time of meetings, or in implementing it once back home. We can be overcome by unbidden doubts, fears, or an inability to act; that is when the C.R.A.S.H. state can paralyze us and prevent us from taking action. Mutual support, in particular, allows us to overcome some of these obstacles and to face challenges with more ease. The facilitator, who works by employing the techniques of collective intelligence, has powerful processes at her/his disposal that will help participants overcome such difficulties more quickly during the group meetings.

Participants also support each other to achieve their goals. Such interactions can take place over the phone, through instant messaging, or, if possible, during face-to-face encounters, if geography and participants' schedules, allow for that. These interactions between group sessions also have the advantage of maintaining a certain kind of rhythm, which is one of the things that make collective intelligence processes successful. Our experience indicates that participants' energy becomes diminished after about six weeks. Maintaining a regular rhythm in the interaction between members is a way of sustaining the group's dynamics. It is important to encourage supportive interaction between people who have different profiles so that the synergies (individual differences and diverse characteristics) can lead to a plentiful emergence of ideas during this stage. Another important advantage of promoting regular interaction at this stage is that members of the group will stay in touch and be supported to come out of their solitude and break with routine. This fosters even more resonance in the group.

Integrating a number of the suggestions we have made in this section serves to catalyze and multiply the results of your Mastermind group. For example, setting an intention by combining multiple forms of intelligence—e.g., words, gestures and images—can be especially helpful.

The authors of this book offer different resources that will allow you to complement what you have learned by reading it. We suggest the following to help you better acquire the know-how that is required to be a facilitator for Mastermind groups where collective intelligence emerges:

* Training that will allow you to become certified for the new profession of collective intelligence facilitator.

* Special training that will prepare you to facilitate Mastermind groups.

* Days of discovery when you can have the experience of and create your own Mastermind group.

* Your own participation as a member of a Mastermind group.

All of the above should allow you to accelerate your own success as you create your own group.

Conscious Leaders Mastermind

The Conscious Leaders Mastermind is an exclusive, accelerated
growth program for successful entrepreneurs and business owners.
The Conscious Leaders Master-

mind integrates the seven core strategies shared by the world's most successful people with the practices of conscious leadership. This provides
participants with a clear roadmap for sustainable success, accelerated
growth, and positive impact (see Chapter 1, pp. 66-71). Current members
include influential leaders from a variety of fields who have positively im-
pacted the lives of hundreds of millions of people.

Conscious Leaders Mastermind was created by author Robert Dilts,
Mitchell Stevko (a Silicon Valley growth expert who has helped over 150
entrepreneurs achieve their dreams, raising over $5 billion in capital) and
Dr. Olga Stevko (a Russian MD and Belief Medicine expert who specializ-
es working with high level professionals). The Conscious Leaders Mastermind program is available only by approved application and interview or
member referral.

If you are ready to take your business and your abilities to an entirely new level of impact and influence, you can learn more and apply for
membership at:

E-Mail: mitchell@consciousleadersmm.com

Homepage: http://www.consciousleadersmm.com

About the Illustrator

Antonio MEZA

Antonio Meza has been drawing cartoons ever since he can remember, but his professional cartoonist work started only recently in his life.

A native of Pachuca, Mexico, Antonio is a Master Practitioner and a Trainer of Neuro-Linguistic Programming (NLP). He has a degree in Communication Sciences from Fundación Universidad de las Américas Puebla, a Masters degree in Film Studies from Université de Paris 3 –Sorbonne Nouvelle, a diploma in Cinema Scriptwriting from the General Society of Writers in Mexico (SOGEM), and a diploma in Documentary Films from France's École Nationale des Métiers de l'Image et du Son (La Fémis).

He participated in animated cartoons startups in Mexico before moving to France where he currently works as a consultant, coach, and trainer, specializing in creative thinking and collective intelligence.

Antonio is also an experienced public speaker and member of Toastmasters International. In 2015 he was awarded best speaker at the International Speech Contest of District 59, covering South-West Europe, and reached the semifinals at the international level.

His cartoons and illustrations have been published by the Université Pantheon-Assas (Paris 2), he co-authored three books (as illustrator); two with Jean-Eric Branaa: "English Law Made Simple" and "American Government Made Simple" published by Ellipses in Paris and "Les Vrais Secrets de la Communication" with Beatrice Arnaud.

He also uses his skills as a cartoonist and trainer to collaborate in seminars, conferences and brainstorming sessions as a graphic facilitator, and to produce animated videos to explain complex information in a fun way.

Antonio has illustrated the three volumes ofs the *Success Factor Modeling* series in collaboration with Robert Dilts, books from which many drawings were borrowed for this book.